WHY ARE PRESBYTERIAN CHURCHES GROWING?

(The Story of Fifteen Thriving Presbyterian Churches)

FOSTER H. SHANNON

GREEN LEAF PRESS, INC.
Alhambra, California

Library of Congress Control Number: 2009903206

ISBN 978-0-938462-05-7

GREEN LEAF PRESS, INC.
P. O. Box 880
Alhambra, California 91802-0880
www.gogreenleaf.com

Printed in the United States of America

OTHER BOOKS BY THE AUTHOR

The Growth Crisis in the American Church

God Is Light

The Green Leaf Bible Series

The Major Themes of the Bible

Seven Strong Reasons Why You Should Believe in Jesus Christ

So You Want To Study The Bible

The Scroll With Seven Seals

But you are a chosen race, a royal priesthood, a holy nation. God's own people in order that you may proclaim the mighty acts of him who called you out of darkness into his marvelous light.

1 Peter 2:9

This book is dedicated to the Pastors and Staffs of these fifteen churches

TABLE OF CONTENTS

INTRODUCTION

The purpose of this book is to inspire, encourage, and teach. In 2005 and 2006, when I was between teaching and preaching assignments, we made it a point to visit other Presbyterian churches in Southern California. We were quite impressed with a number of churches that we visited—and the idea grew on me that there was a story to be told about selected Presbyterian Churches in California. There are about 540 Presbyterian Churches in the state, thus, at least five percent of the Presbyterian Churches in the USA are in the state of California. Of that number fewer than thirty had shown any increase in membership in the five year period of this study, 2002 - 2007. I believed that our sample is large enough so that we could learn lessons that would apply and be instructive to the denomination as a whole. Since we are studying churches that are attempting to follow Jesus Christ—there is a great deal here for Protestant churches generally. Since I live in the Los Angeles area, the logistics were, of course, easier for me to concentrate on one state. Since the Presbyterian churches in Hawaii are a part of the Presbytery of the Pacific (Los Angeles area), they were included in the study. Thus, early in 2007, I began a study with the intention of producing a book.

The former United Presbyterian Church (USA) had been in membership decline since 1966, and with the merger with the Presbyterian Church US in 1983, that membership decline has continued. (Please see the Appendices for details) Indeed, membership decline has been common enough in many Presbyterian churches so that we should take care that we do not grow accustomed or even become comfortable with membership decline. Surely, it is helpful to be reminded that this is not the case with all Presbyterian churches. A significant number of them continue to increase in membership. In this book we highlight fifteen churches in California that have shown an impressive percentage of membership growth in the five year period, 2002-2007.

We understand that God calls us to faithfulness, and that fidelity to our Savior may be exhibited in a number of ways. We further understand that excellent ministries are being conducted, yet, for good reasons, there is no demonstrable membership growth. However, we also understand that a central part of the church's mission is to make our Savior and his gospel known and to call people to faith in him. Here are fifteen churches that give us a good example in the area of evangelism and outreach. Their success in outreach can be an encouragement to the rest of us, and may be a help and an enablement to many of our churches. The last thing that we want to do as a result of this book is to encourage some form of one-upmanship. Tennis players can learn from other tennis players; swimmers can learn from other swimmers, runners can learn from other runners. Surely many of our churches can learn from those who are excelling in Christian outreach!

With few exceptions, these churches have either remodeled their chancels or the entire sanctuary including the chancel. Some have built new sanctuaries. I realized that the traditional style of chancels in Presbyterian and Reformed Churches was influenced by and frequently was an imitation of the sanctuaries and chancels of John Calvin and John Knox during the 16th Century A.D. An increasing number of our ministers no longer attempt to dress as did Calvin or Knox! We now have sophisticated sound and visual systems and a variety of styles of music that were not a part of the sixteenth century. While some contemporaries may seem to go to extremes in their style of music or design of sanctuaries, it surely is no longer appropriate to maintain a rigid loyalty to the styles of Reformed Churches of the sixteenth and seventeenth centuries! Most of us furnish our homes somewhat differently than was the case in the America on the Atlantic shores in the seventeenth and eighteenth centuries. Wooden pews may be traditional for our churches, but also may be anachronistic.

The stories that follow of these fifteen churches are exciting. We see churches that have developed well in the setting in which they find themselves. We see churches that have a strong belief in their ministries and objectives. Surely we have a story here that can be of help and encouragement to many churches in the United States. We remember that we are looking at the work of God as it manifests itself in our presence.

CHAPTER ONE

Bidwell Presbyterian Church
201 West First Street, Chico, California 95928
Tel: 530-343-1484 FAX: 343-7990
www.bidwellpres.org Sacramento Presbytery

Evening view of Church exterior

61% MEMBERSHIP GROWTH, 2002-2007

Year	Members	Gain	%	Lost	%	Wor.Atten.	Receipts
2007	1236	97	8	14	1.1	1000	1,460,780
2002	754	119	13.4	71	10.7	525	827,146
Difference	482					475	633,634

Christian Education Enrollment = 2000

SUNDAY WORSHIP
8:00 a.m.   Traditional Worship
9:30 a.m.   Contemporary Worship
11:00 a.m. Contemporary Worship
5:45 p.m.   Alternative Worship (College). Dinner is provided.

MINISTRY STAFF

Rev. Steve Schibsted	Head of Staff
Rev. Greg Cootsona	Assoc. Pastor, Adult Discipleship
Rev. Jeff Gaphart	Assoc. Pastor, University/Missions
Rev. Jim Coons	Assoc. Pastor, Youth
Bill Hammond	Director of Worship & Arts
Kristin Gephart	Director of Children's Ministries

13 Full Time and 30 Part Time Staff

The Bidwell Presbyterian Church was organized in 1868 as Chico Presbyterian Church. The campus of California State University at Chico is adjacent. It is a downtown church with a building that was constructed in 1931. The building has gone through a recent substantial remodeling and improvement program from 2005 to 2008. The parking lot has a capacity of 40 cars. It attained a peak membership of 1,396 in 1959 and slowly lost members to a low of 419 in 1995. In the past eleven years worship attendance has increased from 295 to almost 1000 on Sundays. Easter and Christmas peaks reach about 1,500. Senior Pastor, Steve Schibsted began his ministry with the church in 1998 and Associate Pastor Greg Cootsona in December, 2002. Pastor Cootsona told much of the story of the church in a booklet published by Geneva Press in 2007, "The Church of the Last Stop." It was distributed to 30,000 Presbyterian church leaders as a part of *The Price H. Gwynn III Church Leadership Series.* Information derived from that book has been incorporated in this chapter. They call themselves The Church of the Last Stop because they are frequently reaching people who have been burned out and stopped attending church. They have impressive numbers of adult baptisms.

The city of Chico is located about ninety miles north of Sacramento. According to Associate Pastor Cootsona, "Chico is essentially an island surrounded by almond orchards and the foothills of Mount Lassen, there are not many other towns from which to draw members." "The City of Chico was founded in 1860 by General John Bidwell, and incorporated in 1872. With recent annexations, the City of Chico has grown to...a Charter city of 86,949 with an urbanized, unincorporated area immediately adjacent to it making the total population of the urban area 105,975 as of 1/1/2008." [From the City of Chico Web Site] Chico is located in a rich agricultural area. The leading crops are almonds and rice along with kiwis, olives, peaches, and plums. Data from the 2000 Census: The population was 82% white (including 13% Hispanic), 2% Black, 4% American Indian, with approximately 12% Asian and other races.

W.O.W. (What's on Wednesdays)

A series of short term classes of about five or six weeks in length led by the pastors of the church on Wednesday evenings. Dinner is provided from 5:30 to 6:30 and the classes run from 6:30 to 7:45 p.m. The series with varying themes is offered five times a year. It is introduced with a Starting Point Lunch including an opportunity to meet the church staff with a program that lasts less than an hour. Registration is required and may require a small fee for materials. A sample of one series follows:

"Gifts & Call" facilitated by Pastor Steve Schibsted. "...provides an opportunity to intentionally and reflectively discern how God has wired you, and gifted you to serve His church and His world."

"Getting To Know God" facilitated by Pastor Greg Cootsona "We will look at key spiritual disciplines such as prayer, reading Scripture, service, tithing, worship, and fellowship."

"Israel's Hopes and Humanity's Deepest Dreams" facilitated by Allen McCallum. "The course explores 6 themes: 1) Getting the Kingdom Started 2) Startling Surprises 3) Longing for a King 4) Why Did Jesus Die? 5) Who Was Jesus? 6) The promise of Easter.

"Pascal Pensees" facilitated by Pastor Dan Barnett. "In this WOW class we'll explore Pascal's life, his famous wager about the faith, and his defense of Christianity".

Side view of Sanctuary after service

11

"Parenting and Teaching" facilitated by Pastor Steve Koch. A program developed by Jim Fay and Foster Cline "learning how to apply the rules of Love and Logic in simple, manageable segments."

CHURCH MEMBERSHIP CLASSES are offered in two formats: 1) as a part of the core class program three times a year and 2) on two days, Fridays 6 - 9 p.m.; Saturdays 9 - 2 p.m.; also three times a year.

REAL LIFE GROUP

These are designated as sermon study and discussion groups. They meet for ten weeks three times a year at various times and places. Study guides are available to attendees on line.

MISSIONS

"Mission is an important area of focus and growth for our congregation, we believe it is imperative that each of us has a greater understanding of what we are doing as a church to respond to God's call, right here in Chico and around the world." The church has reached a goal of giving well over 10% of the operational budget to missions. Mission trips are planned each year to Albania, Haiti, and Mexico—a trip to Swaziland is under consideration. In addition to involvement in local mission projects, the church focuses on these outside of the United States: New Life Homes, Swaziland; Foundation for the Children, Haiti; Albanian Christian Student Group; Albanian Alongside Ministries; Agros, A partnership named "Amigos de Bidwell" that brings the church close to people who are passionate about transforming their lives. The College Program is involved locally with a partnership with another church in Chico. "Students have built relationships in their recovery ministry that supports and houses individuals who are recovering from drug and alcohol addiction."

WOMEN'S MINISTRIES

Presbyterian Women Bible Studies
Presbyterian Women General Luncheon
Prayer Quilt Ministries
Baby Blanket Ministry

MEN'S MINISTRIES

Men who participate in this ministry have the opportunity to discover:
- A personal relationship with Jesus Christ
- Honor Jesus Christ through worship, prayer and to hear God's Word

- Pursue relationships with other men, understanding that every man needs brothers to help keep him accountable.
- Build strong marriages and families through love, protection and biblical values.

COLLEGE MINISTRY (The Door)

Bidwell Presbyterian is adjacent to the campus of California State University at Chico and focuses its outreach program to the college campus. The Alternative Worship Service at 5:45 p.m. on Sundays is an important part of the college ministry.

YOUTH MINISTRIES

- 5th and 6th Grade News & Events meet every Sunday morning during two services: 9:45 a.m. and 11:11 a.m.
- Junior High News & Events (The Underground) meet Wednesday evenings from 6:30 to 8:00.
- High School News & Events meet every Wednesday night from 7:00 to 8:30 p.m.

Brian Solecki is Director of Youth Ministries. He is assisted by Brian Wainwright 5th to 8th Grade Coordinator and by three interns in the 5th and 6th, Junior High, and High School ministries.

Worship Service

CHILDREN'S MINISTRY

"Kidwell Park is the Children's Ministry of Bidwell Presbyterian—a place where kids are treasured and seen as gifts from God, and where they can develop and explore a deeper relationship with Jesus as their "forever friend".

Pastor Schibsted said that he was alerted in a seminary program on how to turn a church into a "missional church"—a church that is looking outward rather than inward. A church has to answer the question: What are we here for? It needs to be sensitive to people; to believe that its mission is for the people who are not yet there. He believes that if a church is going to grow that the people and staff have to be willing to change some things and that can be a difficult and challenging experience for a congregation. Pastor Schibsted and his staff are committed to doing things well; to raise the level of excellence in everything that the church does. He recognizes that people are used to good facilities, thus, fixing up the property needs to be a priority. Good theology makes a difference Growth comes primarily from people who bring their friends. The heart of the church is good worship. People need to feel that they are meeting God. Preaching needs to be understandable and practical; real and passionate. We need to meet people where they are, thus, three styles of worship are offered: Traditional, Contemporary, and a Sunday Evening Contemporary Program designed for young adults. The church needs functional structures. The Session, which meets monthly sets the parameters for ministry and holds the staff accountable—but with that guidance allows for innovation and flexibility in the day to day ministry.

SUMMARY

The Bidwell Church is in an historic downtown setting. It did not relocate. It must rely on street parking for those who attend. It has a strong continuing emphasis on educating its people. It is a good example of staff with complementary gifts working well together. It is a prime example of a traditional church that has successfully gone through renewal.

CHAPTER TWO

Trinity Presbyterian Church
12168 N. Willow Avenue, Clovis, California
559-433-0584; FAX 559-433-0585; E-mail: connect@trinitypres.com
www.trinitypres.com San Joaquin Presbytery

Front view of Church facilities

27% MEMBERSHIP GROWTH, 2002-2007

Year	Members	Gain	%	Lost	%	Wor.Atten.	Receipts
2007	496	19	4	8	2	465	1,724,670
2002	390	46	17	6	2	415	1,073,046
Difference	106						651,624

Sunday Morning Schedule

8:30 and 10:30 a.m.	Sunday Morning Worship Services Blended
8:45 and 10:30 a.m.	Children's Sunday School
10:30 a.m.	Youth Sunday School
10:30 a.m.	Youth Worship (Junior High & High School)
10:30 a.m.	Adult Classes

ABOUT CLOVIS

The city of Clovis began as a freight stop along the San Joaquin Valley Railroad. It is located in the northeast quadrant of the Fresno-Clovis Metropolitan Area and in the agriculturally rich San Joaquin Valley of California. Clovis was incorporated in 1912 with the title, "Gateway to the Sierra." It covers more than 23 square miles in area. The current population is estimated at 94,000 and has more than doubled since 1985. Clovis is situated midway between Los Angeles and San Francisco. In the 2000 Census the racial makeup was 76% white (including 20% Hispanic), 2% Black, 1.5% American Indian, 6.5% Asian, 14% other or mixed.

FACILITIES:

The Church is situated on a 22 acre parcel in the growing north end of Clovis, which is in the greater Fresno metropolitan area. The buildings are new in a contemporary style appropriate to California. Because the Church is situated on a large parcel of land ample parking is available near the buildings. The sanctuary opens to a large patio. In 2003 the "Building for New Life' project completed the first phase of Construction: a 16,000 sq. ft. Worship and Children's Ministry Center. Future phases will include a permanent Worship Center, Family Life and Youth Center, Retreat Center, Amphitheater, and outdoor Sports and Activities Park.

BACKGROUND

"In the summer of 1990, a group of fifty people responded to an invitation to form the core group of a new congregation. They held their first public worship service at Lincoln Elementary School, Palm Sunday, March 23, 1991. On Sunday, June 8, 1997, the Trinity congregation extended a call to Pastor Chuck Shillito to become its new pastor. Along with his wife, Cathy, and their five children, Chuck began his ministry on September 1, 1997.

In 1999 the Long Range Planning Team completed a comprehensive site plan, which received unanimous approval from the County Planning Commission. In April, 2000, God gave us our Building for New Life miracle, with $1.5 million committed and then given by the congregation over the next three years. The former sanctuary was expanded to accommodate growing worship attendance. New parking spaces and office space were added, and construction on the new 16,000 square foot Worship & Children's Ministry Center was completed for Palm Sunday, April 13, 2003. Pay-off of the $850,000 debt on the 22 acre property soon followed."

We attended the worship services during the Advent season. The Narthex had attractive Christmas decorations. The sanctuary had simple but appropriate decorations: 12 poinsettias up front, Christmas trees with tiny white lights, and garland around the top of the room with white lights. Praise Band: (Piano, Trumpet, Drummer, Violin, 2 Guitars, 3 or 4 singers) Excellent view screen on the front chancel wall at the center that was used in connection with a missionary report and primarily for scripture verses during the sermon. No Pews—Attractive and comfortable single chairs. No organ in evidence. A single major Choir Anthem with instruments, "O Holy Night"; an excellent male soloist Sermon by Pastor Shillito: Advent message beginning with the birth of Jesus including a strong emphasis on the prophets and Jesus' second coming. A one page bulletin insert included the key scripture text with the three main points with accompanying scriptures and space for a few notes. The sermon ended with a Bill Gather trio singing "The King is Coming". 8:30 a.m. service appeared full; 10:30 a.m. service about 3/4 full.

Pastor Shillito was notable in being generous with his time greeting and conversing with people as they exited the sanctuary. After the service there were a selection of coffees, a variety of teas and hot chocolate, plus a generous spread of pastries. We found the people friendly and easy to talk to. No charge for refreshments.

Worship Service

STATED PURPOSE:

- Magnify God
- Guide people to Christ
- Equip believers for ministry
- Demonstrate God's love in the world

WEEKLY CALENDAR

Monday	Tae Kwon Do Club, 5:00 p.m.
Tuesday	Staff Prayer Time, 8:45 a.m.; Staff Meeting, 10:00 a.m.; Junior High Youth Group, 6:45 p.m.; College/Young Adult Ministry, 7:30 p.m.
Wednesday	Tae Kwon Do Club, 3:00 p.m.; Worship Choir Rehearsal, 6:30 p.m.; High School Youth Group, 6:45 p.m.
Thursday	Senior Men's Morning Bible Study at Perko's; Sister Talk Book Club, 9:00 a.m. & 6:45 p.m.; Brother Talk Book Club 6:45 p.m.
Friday	Men's Friday Morning Fellowship, 6:00 a.m.

Ministry and Support Staffs:

Chuck Shillito	Sr. Pastor/Head of Staff
Don Harris	Minister of Discipleship
Ed Cobb	Director of Worship and Arts
Deanna Allen	Director of Children's Ministries
Joan Davis	Receptionist/Administrative Assistant
Don Harris	Minister of Discipleship
Cathy Ross	Executive Assistant to the Pastor
Ruben Mejia	Custodians
and Eric Freeman	

The Part-time Staff covers the following areas:

Women's Ministries Assistant, Director of Women's Ministries, Junior High Ministry Coordinator, AV Worship Assistants, Asst. for Pastoral Care/Missions, Newsletter Editor, Business Administrator, High School Ministry Coordinator, College/Young Adult Ministry, Admin. Assistants Sunday Morning Child Care Coordinator, Youth Ministries Assistant Finance Assistant.

Church Membership Classes are held two or three times a year; either a full day on Saturday or a series of four to six classes on Sunday mornings.

Patio between services

SUMMARY

Pastor Shillito and the Trinity Church congregation (with the help of San Joaquin Presbytery) have been exemplary in their planning and faith in God for the future of the church. The choice of the site was audacious because it looked forward to the northward growth of the community. The building program exemplifies careful and visionary planning and strong commitment on the part of the people in the church. Another characteristic of Pastor Shillito and pastors of these fourteen other churches: their dreams for their churches were bigger than they were. They realized early on that they could not do the task by themselves, and exhibited impressive skill in the development of full and part-time staff. The following statement by Pastor Shillito is significant: "I have learned over the years that people will develop an appetite for what you feed them. If you build a church on programs, people will have a hunger for programs. If you build it on entertainment, people will have an appetite for entertainment. But if you build a church on the teaching of God's Word, then people will have an appetite for God's Word. For that reason, the Bible will always be the foundation and centerpiece of all we say and do at Trinity."

CHAPTER THREE

Healdsburg Community Church

(Presbyterian and Methodist) Presbytery of the Redwoods
1100 University Street, Healdsburg, California 95448
707-433-8886 E-mail: jordanirwin@comcast.net
www.healdsburgcommunitychurch.com/

Inside of Sanctuary

19% MEMBERSHIP GROWTH, 2002-2007

Year	Members	Gain	%	Lost	%	Wor.Atten.	Receipts
2007	166	14	85	8	5	187	367,024
2002	140	12	8.5	10	7	158	225,222
Difference	26					29	141,802

Sunday School Attendance = 140 (Beginners - Adult)
9:30 a.m. Blended Worship Service

Staff

Dr. Dave Jordan-Irwin,   Co-Pastor
Dr. Becca Jordan-Irwin,   Co-Pastor
Rev. Roxanne Lemereis,   Minister of Christian Formation
Rev. Dean Anderson,   Minister of Creative Arts in Worship

20

Susan Nelson,   Administrative Assistant
Carlene Sumner,   Choir Director
Carol Finwall,   Financial
Five other part-time assistants

The city of Healdsburg was founded in 1857 by Harmon Heald and incorporated in 1867. It is located 65 miles north of San Francisco. The population is estimated at 13,000. It is in Sonoma County which has an estimated 2007 population of 464,000. County Demographics: White, 70%; Hispanic, 23%; Asian, 4%; Black 1.7%, American Indian 1.5%.

The Healdsburg Church was founded during the 1860s and has been a federated Presbyterian and Methodist Church since the mid-1930s. The preponderance of membership has been on the Presbyterian side. Recently the church has changed its name from Healdsburg Federated Church to Healdsburg Community Church. The church is prominently located on University Avenue which is a main street in Healdsburg.

A few excerpts from the Home Page of the church's Web Site:

"One of the best ways to get acquainted with us is to join us on a Sunday morning. You are also welcome to check out any number of Bible Studies or small groups that are both on-going and seasonal....We know from what the Bible tells us that the church is not where we go; it's who we are....People come together and are united in a way unlike anything they'll ever see anywhere else. United not because they look, act, think, and dress alike, but because they share the same Lord and the same extraordinary purpose to glorify God and build up the church."

We attended the 9:30 a.m. worship service. The church has future intentions of establishing a second service. The sanctuary was well filled (but not completely) with about 200 in attendance. The service was blended with some familiar praise songs. The Order of Worship for this service was as follows: Prelude, Welcome, Children's Song (I'm Gonna Tell The World), Greeting One Another, Praise Song (Open the Eyes of My Heart), Call To Worship, Praise Song (Everlasting God), Prayer, Praise Song (In The Secret), Offering, Gospel Reading, Children's Message, Pastoral/The Lord's Prayer, New Testament Reading, Sermon, Praise Song (Amazing Grace-My Chains Are Gone), Benediction, Postlude. A projection screen is used in the worship service. The Sunday that we attended it was used only for projecting the words to the songs and hymns. Pastor Dave said that he sometimes uses it to illustrate his sermons, but does not put outlines on the projection screen.

The church was at a low ebb with fewer than 100 in worship, and very few children in Sunday School when the Jordan-Irwins began in 1998. They both began as half-time Co-Pastors. Dave was later increased to full time, and additions were made to the staff of the church. Since the 1930s the church has been Federated with a Methodist and a Presbyterian congregation. However, Federated was replaced with Community, because it was recognized that Federated is not a well understood term. The church built an educational unit a few years ago for about $250,000 utilizing a lot of volunteer labor. The debt on the educational unit has been virtually paid off. They promote and plan a Vacation Bible School in cooperation with a Roman Catholic and an Episcopal church—with the majority of children coming from the Community Church.

Some of the courses and studies provided by the church:
The Alpha Course
Natural Church Development
50 days of Spiritual Adventure
Bible study series on the books of John, Ephesians, The Holy Spirit, I John, Women of the Bible, Judges
Men's and Women's Retreats

The Stephen Ministry Program has been a strong emphasis in the church since 2001. About six leaders have completed the intensive 40 hour intensive training course and a new class of seven has completing training. Stephen Ministers have provided over 500 hours of one-to-one Christian caring support for those in crisis. The leadership group meets twice monthly for continuing education and small group supervision.

What is unique about this church?
One senses that the co-pastors, husband and wife, work very well as a team, with a genuine love for their congregation. Their devotion is to the Lord and to the people in the church, and to each other. The church is involved in a number of ministries in the community including: the Healdsburg Shared Ministries Food Pantry, Redwood Gospel Mission, the Manna House and the Pregnancy Counseling Center. Their most recent outreach program is an English as Second Language Course for Hispanic people currently with 17 students and 12 members of the church trained to be tutors. Free childcare is provided for the attendees.

From the Pastors
"We have a very loving and caring congregation. Many of our members are using their gifts to help build up the Body of Christ in Healdsburg. Our older members have been very open to change, and have

been very positive and encouraging about the changes we have made in the worship service. For example, they participate with the sign language for our children's songs. They love the drama presentations and they enjoy the media presentations as well. We knew that younger members of the church would enjoy these aspects in worship, and we are delighted that our long-term members have been supportive.

We also have very generous members in the congregation who continue to support the church with their financial gifts. This has enabled us to build our new Christian Growth Center and develop new programs for the church. Above all, we give all thanks to Jesus who alone has enabled our church to grow and flourish, the power of the Holy Spirit at work in our congregation is the reason we have flourished. Thanks be to God.

We know that the blessings and growth that we have experienced in our church is only because of Jesus and the strength and guidance that we are given daily by the work of the Holy Spirit. We thank God for the many men and women He has raised up to serve in leadership. We truly desire every member to utilize their gifts so the Body of Christ is built up in our community—so that we can share the love of Christ to the people in our area who so desperately need to hear the good news of Jesus. We thank God for the wonderful, loving, generous, gifted individuals in our congregation who deeply desire to serve God with their whole hearts, soul, mind and strength. What a blessing to serve alongside them for the praise of God's glory."

At the Entrance of the Church

ABOUT THE CO-PASTORS

Dave Jordan-Irwin was raised in California. With his family he attended church when he was young but came to full faith in Christ through the ministry of Fellowship of Christian Athletes during his junior year in high school. He graduated from U.C. Santa Barbara with a major in biological sciences. He received the M.Div. and D. Min. degrees from Fuller Theological Seminary. He and his wife Becca began their ministry at Healdsburg Community Church in 1998.

Becca Jordan-Irwin was raised in Colorado and graduated from the University of Colorado. While at the University she was involved with the Fellowship of Christian Athletes and Inter Varsity Christian Fellowship. For a time she worked as a staff member of Fellowship of Christian Athletes. With her husband, Dave, she served as Co-pastor of the Lemoncove, CA Presbyterian Church before coming to Healdsburg.

SUMMARY

Like the Bidwell Church, Healdsburg Community Church is an older, settled congregation that has gone through a decade of renewal. Especially in this case, the fresh leadership and perspectives of David and Becca Jordan-Irwin have been vital. They have brought the congregation through a period of change and growth in such a manner that it appears the congregation is pleased with the current results and the prospects for the future.

Ready for Baptism in the Russian River

CHAPTER FOUR

First Presbyterian Church Of Honolulu
45-550 Kionaole Road, Kaneohe, Hawaii 96744
808-532-1111; FAX 808-532-1112; E-mail aloha@fpchawaii.org
www.fpchawaii.org Presbytery of the Pacific

Front view of the Church facilities

15% MEMBERSHIP GROWTH, 2002-2007

Year	Members	Gain	%	Lost	%	Wor.Atten.	Receipts
2007	1,180	90	7.6	64	5.4	1,147	2,842,017
2002	1,023	133	13.0	22	2.0	877	1,827,246
Difference	157					270	1,104,771

Sunday Morning Schedule

8:00 a.m.	Worship Service
	Sunday School
	Children's Church
9:30 a.m.	Worship Service
	Nursery/Preschool
	Children's Church
	Adult Classes
11:00 a.m.	Nursery/Preschool
	Children's Church

Adult Classes
11:11 a.m.   Contemporary Worship Service

The Sermon is broadcast Sundays at 10:00 a.m. on KGU, 760 AM

PASTORAL AND PROGRAM STAFF

Dr. Dan Chan,   Pastor
Dr. David Stoker,   Executive Pastor
Dr. Sim Fulcher,   Associate Pastor
Dr. Drew Hulse,   Associate Pastor
Ron Mathieu,   Executive Director
Dee Dee Lee,   Director of Congregational Life
Dr. Jordan Seng,   Director of Outreach Ministries
Roslyn Catracchia,   Director of Worship & Performing Arts
Katen Makishima,   Director of Children's Ministries

The Rev. Dan Chun has been Senior Pastor since 1994. He received M.Div. And D.Min degrees from Fuller Theological Seminary, a M.A. from USC in Cinema Production, and a B.S. in Communications from Lewis and Clark college. He is an award winning film maker. Dan is confident, modest, and unprepossessing; evidently works well with staff.

The church was initiated by the Presbytery of Los Angeles in 1957. The Keeaumoku Street property was purchased for the first Presbyterian church to be organized on the islands. Initial worshipers meet at the Richards Street YWCA. The new building was completed in 1961. The air-conditioned sanctuary with a seating capacity exceeding 500 provided room for growth. Additional facilities were provided through two subsequent building programs. First Presbyterian became one of the largest churches in the Hawaiian Islands.

First Presbyterian, Honolulu found that it was constrained with totally inadequate parking and an inability to properly handle a growing attendance. They began a property search and, in the process, found a local 24,000 acre golf course available for sale. The purchase was consummated in August, 2006. The extensive building facilities were fairly easily made suitable for a church ministry. The church leases the operation of the golf course and a restaurant (Honey's) as a part of its ministry. An advantage with the new site are facilities for seminars, conferences, and wedding receptions that help the church relate to the community at large.

26

I attended the 9:30 a.m. Traditional Service, and the 11:11 a.m. Contemporary Service. The sermon was the same in both services. Compassion International was a special emphasis and identical presentations for that ministry were made in both services. The 9:30 service lasted 65 minutes; the 11:11 service lasted 75 minutes. There was a choir of about 35 members in the Traditional Service. Both organ and piano were used in the Traditional Service with additional cello accompaniment in parts of the service. Only the piano was used for the Contemporary Service. Robes were not worn. Pastor Chun was dressed casually in a Hawaiian shirt and slacks. He has an informal tone in both services. He uses humor and does a good job of engaging his audience. He is soft spoken, definitely not bombastic—but speaks clearly and is easy to hear. The projection screen centered in the back of the chancel displayed the words of the songs and also the passages of scripture that the pastor referred to. It was not used for power point.

The Praise Team is composed of six members: a leader, soloist; pianist; bongo drums, and three guitarists. They led in the concluding song following the blessing ("They'll Know We are Christian by Our Love"), and in a postlude song in both services, "Great Is thy Faithfulness". The Praise Team led in the Contemporary Service for about 20 minutes, including two prayers. After that the order was the same as in the Traditional Service. The congregation applauded a few times in both services, including the invitation to the offering.

Sunday Morning Contemporary Service

27

CORE VALUES

Authenticity: We believe God works best in our lives when we live authentically - being honest with others about our struggles and joys.

Humility: We believe that the church should exhibit a humility that is open to new ideas with the leading of the Holy Spirit.

Excellence: We believe that excellence honors God and inspires people.

Evangelism: We believe that because the Gospel is worth sharing with others, we should invite people to church. (Includes relational evangelism and invitation to all church events)

Disciplines: We believe we should be engaged in the disciplines of spiritual life for our spiritual growth and maturity. (Includes prayer, worship, fasting, tithing, Bible study.)

Worship: We believe corporate worship should include all aspects of the performing arts to enjoy God and glorify Him. (Includes hymns, drama, praise songs, media, and dance as expressions of praise.)

Small Groups: We believe that Christian community is essential for spiritual growth and develops best in covenant (small) groups.

Spiritual Gifts: We believe we should be actively serving in our areas of spiritual giftedness.

Biblical Literacy: We believe that Biblical literacy should be the life-goal of every Christian. (Includes understanding the Bible and knowing how to study and apply it.)

SEEKERS & JOINERS

In order to become a member of First Presbyterian Church of Honolulu, a class called "Seekers and Joiners" must be attended. It is designed specifically for those interested in membership. Attendance does not obligate a person to become a member of the congregation. The sessions are conducted by Pastor Dan Chun and/or Pastor David Stoker. Childcare is available upon advance request.

BAPTISM

Baptism is an important mark of new life in Jesus Christ. Those who desire baptism must: 1. Believe that Jesus Christ is the Messiah sent by God to save us from our sins 2. Schedule a pre-baptismal meeting with one of the pastors before the scheduled baptism

MISSIONS & EVANGELISM
New Hope International Vision Tours

Members and friends of Honolulu Presbyterian visit significant mission projects throughout the world. Participants go at their own expense.

Pentecostal Assemblies of Tribes (PAOT)

In 2001 First Presbyterian Church of Honolulu became a partner with Pentecostal Assemblies of Tribes, a fellowship of tribal village churches with a base in Chiang Mai, Thailand. The thrusts are to evangelize and plant churches in non-Christian villages, encouraging tribal pastors and training leaders.

Compassion International: The church supports more than 600 children.

Habitat for Humanity

Operation Christmas Child

River of Life- Food for the hungry

Thanksgiving Dinner

Ministry Support: Funding over 25 ministries

ADULT MINISTRIES

Book Club meets second Saturday of each month

Common Grace mentoring team meets one on one with children of Kaneohe elementary School

Community Services supports help to the needy locally, nationally, and abroad

Divorce Care is a weekly seminar and support group for people who are separated or divorced. Meets Thursdays at 6:30 p.m.

Inside the main entrance leading to offices, classrooms, displays, & dining

Grief Share is a 13 week session on grief recovery

Small Groups: Various groups around the island gather weekly for Bible study, prayer, and fellowship. Small groups are relational groups of 5-20 people, that meet regularly in a variety of places including people's homes

Men's Ministries

Women's Ministries

Young Adults and Families

Why is First Prez growing? (Pastor Dan Chun)

    1. Tried to remove all hurdles to growth

    2. Make worship as excellent as possible

    3. Provide a buffet of options for people to learn about Jesus

    4. Seek to raise the bar of excellence

    5. Humility is a core value; otherwise we will not be teachable

    6. Worship is where we reach the most people: the other programs follow.

    7. We have been willing to risk: Moving 10 plus miles from steeple and pews to golf club. We have asked ourselves the question, Would you do anything to reach people for Christ?

    8. Two important symbols: 1) The Carpathia, the only ship to respond to the Titanic. On the way to a Mediterranean cruise was willing to change its mission and adjust its facilities to save survivors of the Titanic. 2) The Lighthouse: We are our brothers keepers

    9. We believe that music should be excellent. Our approach is eclectic: Broadway, Pop Culture, Opera, Hymns, Praise Songs. All should be done well.

SUMMARY

    Most of these fifteen churches have taken notable steps of faith in developing their ministries. First Presbyterian, Honolulu undoubtedly made an especially bold decision in relocating eleven miles from their original site to a dramatically different setting outside of the city limits. Pastor Chun testifies that the first two years brought considerable difficulties. However, the result has been a renewed and refreshed congregation, which is a superb testimony to following through on a courageous decision.

Current staff: 17 Full-time; 6 Part-time; 2 Contractual.

CHAPTER FIVE

Christ Presbyterian Church

20112 Magnolia Street, Huntington Beach, CA 92646
714-968-4940 FAX 714-968-9432 E-mail: churchoffice@cpchb.org
www.cpchb.org Los Ranchos Presbytery

Church Exterior from Magnolia Street

15% MEMBERSHIP GROWTH, 2002-2007

Year	Members	Gain	%	Lost	%	Wor.Atten.	Receipts
2007	632	19	3	14	2	552	1,415,384
2002	549	43	8	18	3.3	485	1,061,129
Difference	83					67	354,255

Worship Services:

8:00 a.m.	Contemporary Service
9:30 a.m.	Contemporary Service
11:00 a.m.	Traditional Service
6:30 p.m.	Cutting Edge Contemporary Service

Sunday School

8:00 a.m.	Nursery up through Third Grade
9:30 a.m.	Nursery through Junior High (closely graded)
	Adult
11:00 a.m.	Nursery through Fifth Grade
	Senior High Breakfast Club
	Adult Education

Staff

Rev. Gary Watkins	Senior Pastor
Rev. William Welch	Associate Pastor
Dean Bobar	Teaching Assistant
Greg Haugh	Minister to College/Young Adults
Rod Andriese	Director of Youth/High School Ministry
Beth Keppel	Children's Ministry Director

Seven full -time and Ten part- time staff

We attended the 9:30 a.m. Contemporary Service and the 11:00 a.m. Traditional Service. The sanctuary seats about 350 people and was virtually full for the Contemporary Service. In fact, attendance has been so strong that the church is beginning a new Contemporary Service at 6:30 p.m. on Sunday evening—encouraging some of those who attend at 9:30 a.m. to switch to the Sunday evening service. The order of worship was as follows: Welcome and News of the Church; Worship With Our Praises; Worship With Our Offerings; The Offertory; Worship With the Word; Worship With Our Praises. The Praise Songs included "Shout to the North", Open the Eyes of My Heart, "We Fall Down", Great is the Lord" in the first set and "Hosanna" and "You are Worthy of My Praise" before the Benediction. There were six members of the Praise Team, a lead guitarist, who also sang, two female vocalists, two more guitars, a keyboard, and a drum. The pastors did not wear robes in either service. They wore slacks and jackets, but no ties. The choir did not wear robes.

Pastor Watkins message was "Getting It Straight" beginning with Jesus encounter with the Sadducees in Mark 12:18-27. He is an excellent preacher, can be easily heard, and does not drop words at the end of a sentence. He is almost casual in his approach and, at least these services, spoke smoothly and clearly without reference to notes. He speaks to the congregation as if they are his friends, but does not hesitate to emphasize biblical truths that may challenge them.

A high school senior girl presented a three minute video produced by World Vision, and then invited members of the congregation to a two hour event (evidently well planned) on a following Saturday to raise funds for World Vision African ministry. This came out of a personal commitment that she had made to help with world ministry.

An assortment of coffees and doughnuts are offered in the patio between and after services. No charge or donation. The church facilities and grounds are impressive. The church website is user friendly, attractive, and complete. It is kept up to date with current news items. The church produces an attractive monthly newsletter, which is also available via the website.

The city of Huntington Beach has a population of about 200,000, and there are about 700,000 people within a five mile radius. With eight miles of accessible beachfront, the city has the largest stretch of uninterrupted beach on the West Coast. Sporting events include the U.S. Open of Surfing, AVP Pro Beach Volleyball and the Surf City USA Marathon. Approximately 37% of the households have an income above $100,000 a year. The city is located 35 miles south of Los Angeles and 90 miles north of San Diego.

House Building Project, Tijuana, Mexico

The church was organized 4 April 1965 with the first meetings at the Joseph Perry Elementary School. Soon the present property was purchased and buildings were completed. Worship services began in the new facilities early in 1967. The first pastor was Gilbert Allen. Donald E. Roberts served as pastor for sixteen years, 1969-1985. The present pastor, Gary J. Watkins was called by the congregation to be pastor 1 August 1987. He has served the church for twenty-one years. He is a graduate of Princeton Theological Seminary. He served as Associate Pastor at Trinity Presbyterian Church in Santa Ana, California until his call to Christ Presbyterian. His passion is to lead people into God's presence and love in their lives. He and his wife, Susan, have been married for 28 years and have two grown children.

Associate Pastor, William Welch is a graduate of Westmont College. He received the Master of Divinity and Doctor of Ministry degrees at Fuller Theological Seminary. He was the organizing pastor of Sierra Vista Presbyterian Church in Oakhurst, California which grew from 40 to 500 in attendance during his pastorate. He has been with Christ Presbyterian since March, 2006. Bill and his wife, Chris have been married for 38 years and have two grown and married daughters.

BASIC BELIEFS (From the Church's Web Site)

We believe and proclaim the Lord Jesus Christ is the only Savior. He is fully God and fully human, born of the virgin Mary by the power of the Holy Spirit. Jesus died on the cross to pay for our sins and rose bodily from the grave to give us new life. Those who put their faith in Him are adopted as children of the Father through his grace alone. Through faith in Jesus Christ we died in Him and in His resurrection rose in Him to be born again as new creations in Christ Jesus. There is no other Name by which we must be saved than Jesus Christ who will return again.

We believe in God the Holy Spirit who is the Lord and Giver of life, who with the Father and Son is to be worshipped and glorified. The Holy Spirit dwells within each believer bringing forth the "Fruit of the Spirit" to make us like Jesus in life, character, joy and holiness. The Holy Spirit comes upon believers with power gifting them and doing the works of Jesus through the believer to proclaim the Kingdom of God. We believe the ministry of the Holy Spirit is to give witness to our Lord, Jesus Christ.

We believe the Scriptures of the Old and New Testaments to be the Word of God and the rule of faith and life. Given by the inspiration of God, they are to be believed and obeyed and through them the Holy Spirit reveals to us who God is and what God requires of us.

We believe the church is composed of all believers who profess faith in Jesus Christ as Savior and Lord. There are several doctrines within Christianity where faithful and intelligent believers differ. We strive to give space for differences on non-crucial issues while building up the family of God in love for one another through the unity of our love for and devotion to our Lord and Savior, Jesus Christ."

PROGRAMS
Children's Choir
Two groups: ages 4 to first grade and grade two to grade five. Both groups will combine as one choir to sing in church and for various outreach events. Rehearsals are each Sunday 11:00 - 11:45 a.m.

Preschool
Church Membership Classes are held three times a year either on a Friday evening and Saturday morning or a series of sessions for five hours on a Saturday. The Church Membership Class includes basic Christianity, faith commitment, life sharing, how to grow in Christ, the sacraments, stewardship, and about the Presbyterian Church (USA).

Trailblazers Meet on Wednesdays from 7:00 to 8:30 p.m.
A program to help fourth and fifth grades have fun together as they build friendships through age appropriate activities, and to be nurtured in understanding and applying God's truths to the issues they are dealing with in their lives through Bible study.

College Students and Young Adults ("The Gathering") 7:30 p.m. on Thursday Nights. A movement of college students and young adults who are searching for answers together and learning what it means to pursue and live for Jesus in this crazy and hectic world. Searchers, skeptics, doubters, disciples, faithful, faithless, all are welcome.

Men's Ministry

Women's Ministry

Alpha Course A practical introduction to Christianity designed primarily for non-churchgoers and new Christians. Ten Tuesday evenings at the church. Dinner is included.

Health Ministry

REASONS GIVEN BY THE SESSION FOR THE GROWTH OF THE CHURCH (2001-2006)
1. The Holy Spirit is present
2. Long term pastor who is a strong leader
3. Strong ministries with children and youth
4. Our pastor invites prayer

5. Men are stepping up to lead
6. The truth of the gospel is boldly preached with love and grace
7. Everyone is expected to grow
8. A wide variety of programs for both men and women
9. The congregation is friendly

SUMMARY

Pastors Watkins and Welch form a compatible and cohesive team who, with the staff, are in harmony regarding the goals of the church. Distinctives would include a strong emphasis on prayer, the Holy Spirit, and depending upon the power of God. Like many of these churches, their outlook is exogenous (including others) rather than endogenous (restricted to growth from within). The new "Bread of Life" program not only fills an important need in feeding needy people in the community on Sunday afternoons but is unifying in that it involves one in six of the people in the church.

One week Surf Camp, Grades 3-6

CHAPTER SIX

St. Peter's By-the-Sea Presbyterian

16911 Bolsa Chica Street, Huntington Beach, California 92649
714-846-6641 FAX 714-846-5901 E-mail: info@stpetershb.org
www.stpetershb.org Los Ranchos Presbytery

Side view looking toward the Sanctuary

14% MEMBERSHIP GROWTH, 2002-2007

Year	Members	Gain	%	Lost	%	Wor.Atten.	Receipts
2007	357	71	20	24	7	243	569,603
2002	311	40	13	33	11	177	438,327
Difference	46					66	131,276

Sunday Worship Schedule: (Child Care provided)
      9:00 a.m.   Traditional worship
      10:30 a.m.   Contemporary worship
As of early 2009 worship attendance is approaching 400 per Sunday.
Sunday School
      9:00 & 10:30 a.m.   Preschool & Children's Sunday School
      9:00 a.m.   Youth Sunday School
      10:30 a.m.   Adult Sunday School/Bethel Class

Average Sunday School Attendance: Kindergarten - Grade 6, 30; Jr. High and High School, 20-25; Adults, 20.

We attended the Traditional Worship Service at 9:00 a.m. and the Contemporary Worship Service at 10:30 a.m. Both services were approximately one hour in length. The sermons were identical, and about 25 minutes. The time difference from some services in other churches was that the music, announcements, and reports took less time. Pastor Grange wore the same attire for both services: slacks and a colorful Hawaiian shirt.

The 9:00 a.m. service consisted of Prelude, Welcome, Announcements, Responsive Call to Worship, Songs of Praise (Majesty, Blessed Be the Lord God Almighty), Prayer of Confession, Choral Response (Under Eagle's Wings), Offering and Offertory, Pastoral Prayer/The Lord's Prayer, Hymn (How Firm A Foundation), Scripture, Message: "Our Unchanging God", Closing Hymn (Immortal, Invisible, God Only Wise), Benediction, Postlude. Piano and Organ were used for accompaniment.

The 10:30 a.m. service consisted of Praise Songs (Come, Now Is the Time to Worship; In The Secret; How Great Thou Art), Welcome, Announcements, Offering and Offertory, Pastoral Prayer, Scripture Reading, Message: "Our Unchanging God", Closing Song (My Redeemer Lives), Benediction, Postlude (A solo repeat of My Redeemer Lives). The Praise Team consisted of a keyboard, two guitarists, a drummer, and a female vocalist. The vocalist has an outstanding and strong voice, and is a great encouragement to the congregation in their singing. Two screens were used in both services of worship to display the words of music, scripture readings and references, and the primary topics of the sermon.

The Sanctuary is in a large multi-purpose room that serves well for a worship service. The building housing the Sanctuary was completed in 2007. The Church is well located and easily seen on Bolsa Chica Street, a major thoroughfare, and close to Warner Avenue, another major thoroughfare. The property encompasses 2.75 acres. The new Family Worship Center containing the multi-purpose room used for worship, a kitchen, restrooms, nursery and four classrooms. A separate building contains the church offices and a third building, part of which was a former restaurant, houses many of the children's and Christian Education activities. There are plans for building a Sanctuary in the future.

OUR VISION

"St. Peter's By-the-Sea is a family of faith that intentionally reaches out to our community with the love of Jesus Christ. Through God's grace, we actively seek to lead our church family and others into a personal relationship with Christ and to nurture that relationship through Spirit-led worship, biblically based teaching, purposeful discipleship and prayer."

OUR PURPOSE

We are called to glorify God in all we do;
Gather as members of Christ's family;
Grow in discipleship;
Give in serving one another, and,
Go as witnesses for Christ.

Pastor's Evaluation

We have focused on being a multi-generational church, expanding ministries and reaching out to people of all ages. We have also added a contemporary style of worship. Perhaps most significantly our preaching and teaching has been focused on presenting the Word of God in such a way that it is relevant and applicable to our every day lives. We have found that people are open to, even hungry for a personal experience of God in their lives. That is what we have intentionally attempted to lead people to.

Sunday Worship in the Sanctuary

Pastor's Vision for Ministry:

"My vision, my mission, my passion is to see individuals meet their full potential in Christ – to experience the love of God in and through Jesus Christ. That's what transformed my life. I've known the transforming power of Christ in my own life, and the focus of my life and ministry is to see that happen in the lives of others. I believe that the Bible is God's owner's manual for life. The goal of my teaching and preaching is to help people apply the truths of the Bible in their lives in practical, understandable ways. I seek to maintain a team-oriented approach to ministry, recognizing that God distributes gifts through the church family. We are most effective as a community of faith when we are all discovering and implementing the gifts God has given to each of us."

Pastor Chris Grange has been Senior Pastor at St. Peters-By-The-Sea since November, 2002. He states, "My passion is for others to experience the love of God through Jesus Christ, because that's what transformed my life." He committed his life to Christ as a young family man. With his wife Helen and their five children, he spent ten years in full-time mission work with Youth With A Mission. in Kona, Hawaii. Chris led Crossroads Discipleship Training schools, and took many outreach teams on 8-10 week mission trips to several countries in Asia, traveling with his family. After graduating from Fuller Seminary , Chris served as executive pastor at First Presbyterian Church, Bakersfield prior to his call to St. Peter's. Worship services were begun for St. Peter's in 1992, and the church was organized 13 September 1993 with 154 members.

The activities for the week are listed in the bulletin as follows:

Sunday   Slo-Pitch League, Team # 2, 5;15 P.M.; Team #1, 6:30 p.m.

Monday   AA (Big Book) 6:30 p.m. High School Beach Day, 10:00 a.m. - 4:00 p.m. Rainforest Prep Party, 6:00 - 9:00 p.m.

Tuesday   ReWind, Middle School Youth Group, 6:00 p.m. Rainforest Prep Party, 6:00 - 9:00 p.m.

Wednesday   Praying Hands Group, 8:15 a.m. Bible Study, Proverbs, 9:30 - 10:30 a.m. ReNu, High School Youth Group, Beach Bonfire, 5:00 p.m. AA, 8:00 p.m.

Thursday   ReSet, College-age Group, 7:00 - 9:00 p.m. Junior High Beach Day, 10:00 a.m. - 4:00 p.m. ReSet, College-Age Group Beach Bonfire, 5:00 p.m.

Saturday   Walking Club, 8:00 a.m. Rainforest Set-up, 8:30 a.m.

Church Staff:

Rev. Chris Grange,	Pastor
Steve Sherrill,	Director of Discipleship &Ministries to Families
Rev.Chris Strutt,	Parish Associate
Adam Reyes,	Youth Ministries
Kathy Gurden,	Children's Ministries
Denyce Budd,	Administrative Assistant
Lynn Silver,	Choir Director
Frankie Lee,	Contemporary Worship
Ron Morse,	Pianist

Coffee Fellowship outside the Sanctuary

SUMMARY

It was a surprise to find two growing Presbyterian congregations in the same city! The two churches are eight miles apart. Their percentages of growth for the five year period were almost identical. It is fair to say that their ministries are somewhat distinctive, but complimentary. The music, sermons, and church programs—while surely faithful to their Savior—are sufficiently distinctive to appeal to a broader audience than either church could alone.

CHAPTER SEVEN

Irvine Presbyterian Church
4445 Alton Parkway, Irvine, California 92604
949-786-9627 FAX 949-786-4312
www.irvinepres.org   Los Ranchos Presbytery

Front view of the Church

13% MEMBERSHIP GROWTH, 2002-2007

Year	Members	Gain	%	Lost	%	Wor.Atten	Receipts
2007	777	63	8	70	9	646	1,839,778
2002	689	92	13.4	74	10.7	643	1,367,229
Difference	88					3	472,549

Christian Education Enrollment = 1,445

Worship Services
9:00 a.m.   Traditional Blended
10:30 a.m.   Contemporary Blended
7:00 p.m.   Veritas, Post-contemporary

Church Staff:

Rev. Rick Hull   Interim Pastor
Rev. Tim Avazian   Associate Pastor
Rev. Kirk Winslow   Associate Pastor for College and Young Adults

The former pastor Dr. Mark Roberts had been with the Church for eleven years. He resigned in 9/30/07 to take a position as Director of the Laity Lodge in Texas. The Rev. Rick Hull began serving as Interim Pastor in November, 2007. Rev. Tim Avazian has been on the church staff for eleven years and Rev. Kirk Winslow for eight years. The church has had two installed senior pastors: J. Ben Patterson and Dr. Mark Roberts who served for sixteen years. On 7 December 2008, the Pastor Nominating Committee was elected to seek the third installed Senior Pastor for the church.

FROM THE MISSION STUDY OF IRVINE PRESBYTERIAN (November, 2008)

Irvine Presbyterian is centrally located in the City of Irvine along one of the major east-west arterials. It is also centrally located in Orange County, California. Current projections have the county exceeding 3.2 million people by 2012. The church draws the majority of it attendants within an area bounded on the west by the 55 freeway; on the north Portola Parkway; on the east by Lake Forest; and to the south the 73 Toll Road. This area represents roughly 81 square miles and includes portions of the communities of Irvine, Tustin, Lake Forest, Laguna Woods, Costa Mesa, and Newport Beach. The current population within this mission area is estimated to be about 275,000.

Inside the mission area are several colleges and universities. The University of California, Irvine, is a major research university. The proximity of these institutions and the strong entrepreneurial spirit found in Orange County are an important part of the local ethos. Orange County is reported to have more than 113,000 millionaire households. The community is affluent and highly educated. The congregation is relatively consistent with the community profile; however, less reflective of the changing racial/ethnic mix in its mission area.

MISSION STATEMENT: "Together, we will follow Jesus as Lord, make disciples, and engage our culture with God's transforming love."
Together: As the triune God, in essence, is community, so also are we called into community, both with God and with one another. By the

power of the Holy Spirit, we participate together in God's mission. (I Peter 2:9)

Follow Jesus as Lord: Jesus called his first disciples with the simple invitation, "Follow me." (Mark 1:17) The amazing journey of abundant life in Christ still unfolds as we respond to those words, becoming disciples of the one at whose name "every knee should bend, in heaven and on earth and under the earth, and every tongue confess that Jesus Christ is Lord, to the glory of God the Father." (Philippians 2:10-11)

Make Disciples: This imperative derives from Jesus' "Great Commission," and urges us to invite everyone to respond to God's grace, and become intentional and growing Christ-followers (Matthew 28:18-20)

Engage our culture with God's transforming love: As we follow Jesus, his love compels us to live, not for ourselves, but for him. By the power of the Holy Spirit at work in and through us, we become his ambassadors to the world in which we live (II Corinthians 5:14-20)...

Patio Between Sunday Services

We attended both the 9:00 a.m. and 10:30 a.m. worship services. There is not a great deal of difference between the two. Both have bulletins with a fairly standard (or formal) listing. The 9:00 a.m. services relied exclusively on the piano, while the 10:30 a.m. added a small praise team of two guitars and a female soloist. It appears that the church does not have an organ.

44

The order of the 9:00 a.m. service was as follows: Piano Prelude, Call to Worship, Song (How Great Is Our God) Guitarist plus piano, Hymn (How Great Thou Art) with piano, Prayer, The Apostles' Creed, Hymn (Be Thou My Vision), Prayer, Solo (The Lord's Prayer), Passing the Peace of Christ, Offering, Offertory (Solo, His Strength is Perfect), The Doxology, Prayer of Dedication, Scripture Reading (Revelation 1:1-11), Sermon by the Rev. Rick Hull, Hymn (Lift High The Cross), Benediction, Piano Postlude.

The 10:30 a.m. service followed a similar order with additional praise songs early in the service, "Let Everything That Has Breath", "Mighty To Save" (instead of "How Great Is Our God"); Child Baptism; Song, Nothing But The Blood of Jesus—in a praise song style (instead of "Be Thou My Vision"). Other than these notations, the services were the same. The first service was one hour in length and the second one hour and five minutes. A projection screen was not used in either service. People are invited to a semi-private prayer area in the front corner of the sanctuary for prayer following each worship service. Pastor Hull was attired in a conservative sport coat, tie, and slacks. The two associate pastors who participated, one in each service, wore shirt and slacks.

Coffee Fellowship in the large patio followed each service with a substantial number of people engaging in conversation and refreshments. A selection of coffees were provided free of charge, and donuts were furnished with a suggested donation of 75 cents. Volunteers staffed Information Booths at both ends of the Patio.

The Church has a New Members Class four times a year. Ordinarily the classes are held on Sundays and run for six weeks. The announcement on the Web Site reads: Basics of the Faith and New Members Class, "Each quarter, a Basics/New members class is offered to those that are interested in learning more about Irvine Presbyterian Church. This class offers a basic overview of the Christian faith, the historical roots of the Presbyterian Church, and practical suggestions on how one can get involved in the life of our church. It is also a great way to meet and connect with people as we seek to be a community of believers who love God, love each other and love our neighbors. Through our time together, you will be able to meet some new friends and establish a stronger connection to our church body. If you are interested in finding out more about IPC or if you have been around and are ready to become a member of our congregation, please e-mail Pastor Tim or call the church office, 949-786-9627 to register for the next class."

The weekly bulletin insert, "Church Life at IPC" gives considerable information on the opportunities for worship, learning, and fellowship. The following classes are offered during the school year: Words for the Wise, Career Counseling, Classic Women, Book Club, Friends in fellowship, The SALT Co. (Single Adults Learning Together). Two adult classes meet on Sunday mornings at 9:00 a.m.: Verbum Dei. This class was studying Rick Warren's book, The Purpose Driven Life, and the Cornerstone Class studying the book of Acts. The church puts out a monthly twelve page newsletter, "Salt Shaker" that includes a calendar page. It is will done with generous use of color. The web-site is attractive, has a user friendly content column on the front page. The web-site is kept up to date.

Other regular activities:
Women's Wednesday Morning Bible Study The September through December session will run for 12 weeks. The cost is $20. Nursery and child care is provided.
Monday Women's PM Bible Study, September 15 to December 1. Cost $15.
Mommie Time, Thursdays, 10:00 a.m.

Entrance to Church on Meadowbrook Street

Ministries:

The 20's Ministry, for persons between ages 20 and 30.

> College Ministry meets each Thursday night from 7:00-9:00 p.m. in the Youth Lounge for fellowship and Bible Study. Also regular social and ministry events.

High School Ministry, Sunday mornings at 10:30 a.m. and Wednesday nights at 7:00 p.m.

SUMMARY: Like most of the churches in this book, one is impressed that the programs and ministries are well planned and carried out. The church appears to tailor its ministries, including the worship services, to an understanding of the community of which it is a part. Yet it seems firm in its commitment to the historic positions of the Christian Church. This church is a good model for presenting classic Christianity in a way that is appropriate to the culture in which it is immersed.

CHAPTER EIGHT

Shepherd Of The Sierra Presbyterian Church
5400 Barton Road, Loomis, California 95650
916-652-4851 FAX 916-652-4895 E-mail: secretary@shepherdpres.org
www.shepherdpres.org Sacramento Presbytery

Shepherd of the Sierra Exterior

18% MEMBERSHIP GROWTH, 2002-2007

Year	Members	Gain	%	Lost	%	Wor.Atten.	Receipts
2007	391	21	5.4	2	0	219	559,000
2002	316	16	5	3	1	228	296,872
Difference	57						162,128

The 10:00 a.m. Sunday worship service is described as blended with both traditional hymns and praise songs. The church previously had two services, and is looking forward to reestablishing a second service. Sunday School Attendance: Approximately 65

THE SHEPHERD OF THE SIERRA is in Loomis, an incorporated town of about 7,000 in Placer County. The County is noted for its Gold Rush heritage. Portions of two National Forests are within its boundaries. The County has a population of about 310,000. The median resident age in Loomis is 38.4 years compared to a California median of 33.3 years.

The median income is higher than that of the state. The population is 85% white. The church draws its members and attenders from an area considerably larger than the town. Loomis is located north of Interstate 80, about 25 miles north-east of Sacramento, and between Rocklin on the SW and Auburn on the NE. It is not on a main road.

Leadership and Staff

Dr. David Ratcliff	Pastor
Rev. David Carroll	Parish Associate
Cathy Lovejoy	Director of Child & Family Ministries
Randy Henry	Director of Youth & Young Adult Ministries
Steve Corey	Associate for Ministry of Music
Barbara Besson	Administrative Assistant
Carol Nielsen	Administrative Assistant

About nine full and part-time staff

Pastor David Ratcliff was raised in the Church of the Nazarene. His father was a pastor in that denomination. He attended Point Loma College in San Diego and the Nazarene Theological Seminary in Kansas City, Missouri. He believes that he was called of God to be a pastor at age 11. He is a Presbyterian by choice. He had previously served two Presbyterian churches before becoming pastor of the Shepherd of the Sierra in 1995. The church was founded in 1986.

The church uses a projection screen in the Sanctuary primarily for the words of songs. During the school year, he does not rely on "Power Point". However for a sermon series in the summer, he will present a 12 week series on "Questions of the Faith" and use power point for that series. It gives him the opportunity to answer questions that the people ask.

Sunday Worship Service, 10:00 a.m. Prelude; Welcome, Pastor David Ratcliff; Song, "Come Into His Presence" (Time of welcoming one another in the name of Christ); Song, "Give Thanks"; Call To Worship, Lay Leader; Hymn, "The God of Abraham Praise"; The Call to Confession, Lay Leader; Unison Prayer of Confession; Time for Silent Confession; Assurance of Forgiveness; Congregational Response, "All Creatures of our God and King"; The Apostle's Creed; Special Music, "Holy, Holy, Holy"; Choir Anthem; Time with Young Disciples; The Written Word: New Testament Luke 14:7-14; Sermon, "Table Talk: Meal Etiquette, Pastor Ratcliffe; Hymn, "Jesus! What a Friend to Sinners!"; Offering and Prayer of Dedication; Offertory; Congregational Response, "Sing Unto the Lord a New Song"; Sharing Joys and Concerns; Prayers of the People (including the Lord's Prayer); Hymn, "We Are Called to Be God's People"; Commissioning to Go and Serve; Friendship Chain, "Shalom"; Postlude. Coffee and Fellowship held in the foyer following the worship service.

Pastor Ratcliff lists eight reasons for the success and well being of the church:

1. Joy-Filled, Christ-centered Worship
2. Commitment to spiritual growth
3. Elders trained as spiritual leaders
4. Active care and love for all
5. Keep focused on the important things
6. Open, accepting environment
7. Passion for Christ
8. Future Oriented

Shepherd of the Sierra is a highly dynamic church that is constantly gaining new members, who bring new talents and ideas. Innovative ideas are welcomed by the pastors and church leaders. People are encouraged to new activities, and since imaginative programs always entail some risk taking—people are not penalized for making mistakes. As a consequence of this participative environment, many creative ideas are implemented by members of Shepherd of the Sierra, as exemplified in church programs, mission activities and the novel uses of facilities. Another factor that contributes to the dynamic environment at Shepherd of the Sierra is that both the congregation and church leaders are willing to make changes as new ideas are implemented. This acceptance of new ideas and willingness to change make Shepherd of the Sierra an exciting place for worship and discipleship. (Pastor Ratcliff)

The Sunday Evening "GIFT Program" is new. It is multi-generational. It is held one Sunday a month with a common meal and planned activities and some separate instructional time. Because many of the families do not share the same organizations and schools, etc.—an important purpose is to emphasize their unity in Christ. The pastor leads two Bible studies on Wednesdays.

From the home page on the website:
SHEPHERD OF THE SIERRA PRESBYTERIAN CHURCH is called by Christ to WELCOME you as a child of God regardless of your background or doctrine EQUIP you to live as Christ has called you with joy, enthusiasm and love SEND you into the world to share the love, compassion and healing of Christ with a world in need.

Main Church Entrance

Shepherd of the Sierra has an attractive website with good color photos (www.shepherdofthesierra.com). It is a source of much useful information about the church, and provides a directory for finding additional information on specific programs.

The Women's Fellowship meets on the second Thursday of every month at 9:30 a.m. Usually the meetings are held at the church. Their main emphasis is Bible study, fellowship, and mission projects. There are also occasional field trips. An active Women's Book Group meets the fourth Friday of every month at 10:00 a.m. in various homes.

The church's Mission Programs emphasize practical help for people: "We believe the natural outgrowth of discipleship is the giving of oneself. We see our community of faith as a gathering of individuals empowered to do the specific ministries to which God has called each. We believe that God is calling us to expand into ministries that can be lived out in our places of work, our homes, our community, and throughout the world. We are committed to reaching out and serving those outside our church. We do this by sharing our facilities and by active involvement with groups in our community." These emphases include: "We join other churches in housing and feeding the homeless year round. During the previous six months over 100 members of our church cooked, served, entertained, and hosted." Mission to the Hungry includes participation in the Two-Cents-a-Meal program, members cooking meals at the St. Vincent de Paul dining room, collecting and distributing food for the Loomis Food Closet, and delivering meals to seniors in Rocklin and Loomis through the Senior Nutrition Program. The church emphasizes the annual one Great Hour of Sharing Offering that is received annually to help people around the world who suffer as a result of disasters such as hurricanes, earthquakes, famine, and infectious diseases. The church produces a monthly newsletter written by Pastor Dave to update the congregation on special events and new developments in the life of the church. Past issues can be viewed on the website and Sermon Downloads are available.

Front of Church Building

CHURCH MEMBERSHIP CLASSES

2½ hours each on two Sunday Evenings; faith sharing among those attending; the background of the Shepherd of the Sierra Church (22 years old) and the Presbyterian Church (USA); video on what it means to be a Presbyterian. The basic resource is a 25 page booklet prepared by the pastor.

SUMMARY

Loomis is not in a major metropolitan area. Those who participate in the church come from a fairly wide area. Several communities and a number of school districts are represented. Opportunity for regular meaningful contacts on the part of the congregation are important. Thus, the recent monthly LIFE program fulfills several needs at the same time including bringing the congregation together in a different setting than worship on Sunday mornings. There are, also, eight small groups meeting during the week.

CHAPTER NINE

Bel Air Presbyterian Church

16221 Mulholland Drive, Los Angeles, California 90049
818-788-4200 FAX 818-788-2243 E-mail: info@belairpres.org
www.belairpres.org Presbytery of the Pacific

View of Sanctuary

45% MEMBERSHIP GROWTH, 2002-2007

Year	Members	Gain	%	Lost	%	Wor.Atten.	Receipts
2007	2693	264	10	55	2.0	2680	7,968,410
2002	1853	207	11	119	6.4	1758	4,298,000
Difference	840					922	3,670,410

Sunday Worship Services

    9:00 a.m.   Traditional
    11:00 a.m.   Contemporary
    6:00 p.m.   Contemporary
Sunday School Attendance: 6208

Sunday School Classes (9:00 and 11:00 a.m.)
> Infants through 2 years
> 2 years through Preschool
> Pre-K through K
> 1st to 3rd Grade
> 4th to 5th Grade
> 9:00 a.m. Middle School ("The Element") 6th to 8th Grade
> 9:00 a.m. High School Bash (9th to 12th Grade)

A variety of adult classes meet on Sunday mornings throughout the year

Program Staff

Rev. Mark Brewer	Head of Staff
Roger Dermody	Executive Pastor
Carolyn Crawford	Pastor of Congregational Life
George Hmman	Pastor of Discipleship
Kimberlee Door	Designated Pastor to Entertainment Industry
Enock De Assrs	Pastor of Outreach

Full Time Support Staff

Communications Director	Director of Children's Discipleship
Traditional Worship Director	Contemporary Worship Director
Director of Finance	Information Services Director
Director Middle School	Weddings & Memorials Director
Director of Young Adults	Plus Managers, Coordinators,
Director of High School	and other support staff
Director of College	

The traditional worship service begins at 9:00 a.m. The organ is prominent and powerful. A large screen was used for the words to the songs, for announcements, and for highlights in the morning message. The order of worship included a powerful organ prelude (Allegro, Symphony No.5, Windor), Welcome and Announcements, Call to Worship, Opening Hymn (Praise to the Lord, the Almighty), Invocation, Song of Worship (Jesus You're the Center, Gaither), Pastoral Prayer, Offering Prayer, Offering, Offertory, Scripture Reading, Brief Video on Jerusalem, Message: "The Jerusalem Dilemma", Closing Song (My Faith Looks Up To Thee), Benediction, Organ Postlude.

The sanctuary was filled for the 11:00 a.m. Contemporary Service. There were very few empty seats. The Praise Band consisted of five guitars (one of them the leader), pianist, drummer, and female vocalist.

The lead guitarist, and some of the other men, sang as well. Occasionally the female vocalist would sing an introductory section or a stanza of a song. The Praise Team is very strong. They command your attention—perhaps, to some degree, override the singing of the congregation. The musicians, obviously, are very good. While their tone is not everyone's cup of tea, it is apparent that they fit, and the congregation is with them.

The service began with announcements (which were also displayed on the screen at the front) by the Executive Pastor, Roger Dermody. He introduced the Jackson family, missionaries involved in linguistic work in Asia, and supported by the Bel Air Congregation. The Praise Band led in three songs: "The Lord God Almighty", "The King of Glory", "Lead Me To The Cross". A time to greet one another in the congregation followed. A brief video was shown on Jews in Israel. The guest speaker was David Brickner, Director of Jews for Jesus, and one of the mission interests of the church. His message was "The Jerusalem Dilemma". He concluded his message leading the congregation in singing, "Blessed Is He That Cometh in the Name of the Lord" in Hebrew and in English. The offering was received with a solo by the female vocalist, "Hosanna", accompanied by the Praise Band. The Praise Band led in the closing song, "Cannons". Followed by the Benediction in Hebrew and English by David Brickner. The service was an hour and ten minutes in length.

Reasons Given For Success of the Church's Ministry

An excellent pastoral staff, An emphasis on small groups, Amazing lay leadership, A heart for reaching out to our city: Our mission is "Making Los Angeles the greatest city for Christ", A love of the Lord, Good solid Bible preaching, Emphasis on Christ as personal Lord and Savior, Encouragement to care for one another and spend time daily in prayer and the word.

Our Philosophy

Bel Air Presbyterian Church is ultimately about making disciples of Christ. A disciple is someone whose behavior and attitudes are being transformed into the likeness of Christ. We focus on making disciples to accomplish a further purpose: to build bridges and partnerships with other churches in and around Los Angeles so that LA becomes known as the greatest city for Christ in America! Transforming people into the likeness of Christ, we encourage our members to grow in three areas:
- Understanding God's Word, and applying it to our lives

- Developing healthy, accountable relationships with other Christians
- Appreciating and exercising our spiritual gifts

Sunday Worship Service

What We Believe
- We believe the Bible to be the inspired, the only infallible, authoritative Word of God
- We believe that there is one God, eternally existent in three persons: Father, Son, and Holy Spirit
- We believe in the deity and humanity of Christ, in His virgin birth, in His sinless life, in His miracles, in His vicarious and atoning death through His shed blood, in His bodily resurrection, in His ascension to the right hand of the Father, in his present rule as Head of the Church and in His personal return in power and glory
- We believe that for the salvation of lost and sinful people regeneration by the Holy Spirit is absolutely essential
- We believe in the present ministry of the Holy Spirit, by whose indwelling the Christian is enabled to live a godly life
- We believe in the resurrection of both the saved and the lost—the saved unto the resurrection of life, and the lost unto the resurrection of eternal separation from God
- We believe in the spiritual unity of all believers in our Lord Jesus Christ

57

The church began as a new church development under founding pastor, Dr. Louis Evans, Jr. about 1958. The congregation consists of persons age 35 and younger, a smaller Boomer population, and a larger group 65-95. Bel Air is a regional church with almost all attendees coming by automobile. Perhaps one-half of the members are related in some way to the entertainment industry.

SOME PERSPECTIVES FROM PASTOR MARK BREWER

This is the fourth large Presbyterian Church that Dr. Brewer has been pastor. He came to Bel Air from Colorado in 2001. While a student at Fuller Seminary he served as an Intern at Bel Air. He complete his seminary training at Princeton Theological Seminary. He sees three basic legs to the ministry at Bel Air: Worship, Christian Education, and Youth. He believes that the small group program has been indispensable to that ministry with 250 to 300 small groups related to the congregation. There are more people in small groups than in Sunday worship attendance. People are frequently introduced to the program via a six week small group program during Lent. The only commitment is for the six week program, but many then become a part of an on going small group. The leaders keep in touch with them via the Internet.

Patio and Buildings opposite Sanctuary

Pastor Brewer sees his time divided in three basic areas: 1) Pastoring 2) Staff and Elders 3) Relating with other churches and the world. He believes that good staff relations are essential to produce a growing church. A primary interest is associating and planning with pastors of churches of a variety of denominations and ethnic groups in the greater Los Angeles area. He views the local church as "base camp", but he says, "You don't live at base camp. Thus, the intentional involvement with other churches in the community to change the city. It takes energy and money, but the commitment raises the spirit of the congregation.

SUMMARY

For a large Presbyterian church a 45% membership growth over a five year period is impressive. One thing we learn from Bel Air is a commitment to excellence in every part of the church's life. One senses that they will not undertake a new phase of ministry unless they believe that they can do it well. Small group programs have been with us for a long time. However, I think this is an area where Bel Air can teach the rest of the church. It definitely is not a sideline; it is large and integral to their ministry. The doctrinal commitment of the church ("What We Believe") is noteworthy.

CHAPTER TEN

Highlands Church
215 Oak Hill Road, Paso Robles, California
Phone: 805-226-5800 FAX 805-226-5801
E-mail: graham@highlandsadventure.org
www.highlandsadventure.org Presbytery of Santa Barbara

New Church Facilities, Opening Sunday, 4 January 2009

467% ATTENDANCE GROWTH, 2006-2008

Average Worship Attendance:
2006 = 147; 2007 = 415; 2008 = 686
2006 Contributions: $79,164
2008 Income: $542,000 (including $100,000 Presbytery support)
Projected Budget for 2009: $622,463 ($70,000 from Presbytery)

WORSHIP SERVICES
Saturday Evening   6:30 p.m.
Sunday Morning   8:30, 9:45, and 11:00 a.m.
All in the new facilities in the Highlands Center, Paso Robles (beginning 4 January 2009)

FULL TIME STAFF

The Rev. Graham Baird   Pastor
Jamie Baird   Director of Outreach;
Caleb Landon   Director of Worship / Arts;
Kay Griffin   Director of Children's Ministries;
Nick Rose   Director of Youth & Family Min.

The Highlands Church began on Easter Sunday, 2006 with 195 in worship; the following week 60 and the week after that 75. The latter part of 2008, 700 or more were present for weekly worship services. The first weekend in 2009 in the Highlands Center 1200 were present for worship and on the second weekend 1000.

The pastor and others leading in worship were casually dressed. Typically Pastor Graham Baird wears jeans, cowboy boots and a good looking shirt. The praise band was good. The leader is a paid member of the staff. Two keyboards, four guitars, and a strong drummer. Two female vocalists.

FROM THE CHURCH'S WEBSITE

"Since Highlands first Sunday at the Park Cinemas Movie Theater in Paso Robles, when we were 30 people strong, our vision has been to help dechurched people become fully devoted followers of Jesus Christ through transformational teaching, committed relationships, genuine prayer and worship, humble servanthood, help for the poor, and the ongoing miracle of people being revolutionized by Christ. We want you to know that wherever you are on your spiritual journey, whether you're just beginning to investigate Christianity or you already have a mature relationship with Jesus, we're here to help you take the next step spiritually and to offer you a place where you can be as involved as you choose. There are four weekend services at Highlands Church in the Highlands Center in Paso Robles. Using multi-media, contemporary music, and a message that connects with people's lives, the ageless wisdom of scripture is presented in a creative, yet straight-forward way. People who haven't attended church, or for some reason have quit going to church, are often surprised at how meaningful these services are. In fact, the services are specifically designed for individuals checking out what it really means to have a personal relationship with Jesus. Even long-time Christians find these series invaluable to their spiritual and personal growth." [The Highlands Church Web-site is attractive, complete, and kept up-to-date weekly]

An emphasis on small group meetings. Keyboard duet with pastor and member of the praise band for the offertory. Very good solo by female vocalist based on a familiar hymn. The motion picture screen was used for power point, mainly background stills plus the main points of the pastor's sermon. The pastor covered a considerable portion of the theater greeting many prior to the beginning of worship

8/3/08: We attended the 10:30 a.m. worship service in the Cinema. The theater is centrally located on the main square of downtown Paso Robles. The service was quite informal, an hour and five minutes in length. The music was led by a strong praise team with three female soloists and a male lead , three or four guitars, a keyboard and a drummer. The quality of the music was very good. Their style could be characterized as "Christian Rock". At times, I thought that the Praise Team overrode the congregational singing, and that it was not always easy to sing along with. Jr. High and High School students are encouraged to attend the worship services. The total attendance at the three services was 700.

Meeting in new Auditorium

The order of worship included: A welcome by the pastor; three praise songs; a brief video on the theater screen on a "Ten Thousand Cans" program sponsored by the church to help supply a local food bank. The message by Pastor Baird, "The Power of Praise" was based on Philippians 1:1-17 (about

62

20 minutes in length). He emphasized care in the words we choose to use; his exhortation was that our words should be a positive as possible. The message was followed by a quiet song and the Communion Service, which the church currently celebrates on a quarterly basis.

PROGRAMS/ACTIVITIES

Baptism class for children ages 8 - 12, three Tuesday evenings, and repeated on a quarterly basis.

Vertical View (Jr. High) every Tuesday 7 - 8:30 p.m.

High School Ministry (Reflect") ninety minutes every Wednesday at 7:30 p.m.

Instead of Vacation Bible School a **Football Camp** with Bible lessons. Attendance in 2007, 120 and in 2008, 135.

Kompass: a training program for high school kids to volunteer in the children's program ages 2-12.

Elements is a program for mothers to come relax and connect the second and fourth Thursday of each month; 9:00 to 10:30 a.m. Programming provided for ages birth to five.

Bible study led by Pastor Baird at Two Little Birds Bakery on Wednesdays from 12:00 to 12:30 p.m. Pastor Baird takes them through a book in the Bible with an attendance of 30 to 40.

Cornerstone (Church Membership) Class was meeting on three successive weeks, but changed in the fall of 2008 to a single meeting three hours on a Saturday morning quarterly: What do we Believe?; The Bible; Who we are and what we believe at Highland. Interested persons sign a list to participate.

Small Group Program Three Saturdays in the Fall, with breakfast, to introduce small group program and assign people to a group of their interest, led by lay people. Some do Bible studies, one does a study based on previous week's sermon, and a variety of other themes.

Women's group every Tuesday night at a large room in a local hotel. 30-35 women in attendance and then divided up by tables with a coordinator at each table.

Lamplighters (senior's program); three couples do planning for activities.

Annual family camp.

Three church-wide picnics at a park, annually.

Easter Service held at Paso Robles Inn in 2008

Easter Services in 2007 outdoors at church property

Two Christmas services at Kennedy Fitness Center (adjacent to the new church facilities) with the large gym filled each time.

WHAT WE BELIEVE (excerpted)

"The mission of Highlands Church is to help dechurched people become more fully devoted followers of Jesus Christ. The sole basis of our belief is the Bible, which is uniquely God-inspired, without error, and the final authority on all matters on which it bears. Our church is built upon the hope and saving grace of Jesus Christ. We believe that Jesus is "the way the truth and the life" and that there really is no other road to health and happiness, balance and wholeness, freedom and eternity except through belief in Jesus Christ. We believe that Jesus is simultaneously both fully God and fully human. The power of Jesus stems from his forgiveness of our sins, his suffering and death while on a cross, his example of love while he was in this world, and most important his resurrection from the dead The nature of God is extremely complex, but essentially consists of three persons in one being (Trinity). God is Father, Son and Holy Spirit...one God....We believe that God created the cosmos out of nothing, fashioned both men and women in God's own image and called creation "good". We believe that humanity was made perfect, and then fell from perfection as a result of its own sinful activity. Ever since humans first sinned, they have lived in a "state of sin". We believe that living in sin is both the hard reality of being human, as well as a daily result of our falling short of the perfection of God."

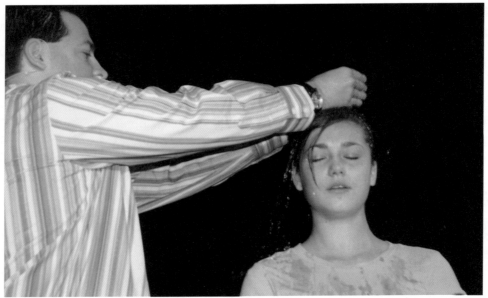

Baptismal Service

64

The Highlands Church has published a summary of ten principles of ministry. The following is substantially abridged:

1. "Who Me?" Leaders: Not looking for a job, Teachable, "Out of the Box", Humble, More often Betas than Alphas, "Not churchy",
2. Personal & Relational: Hand written cards; Phone calls to first time visitors by the Pastor
3. Hire Outside the Box: Quality staff can be found outside the Presbyterian Church (USA)
4. News & Media: The best method of getting the word out about your church is free!
5. Meet People Where They Are: Study and Understand your Community.
6. Minimize name "Presbyterian": Marketing experts emphasize the need to diminish brand names in order to sell a product.
7. Web, Newsletter, Text: Write a Newsletter that can be read in ten minutes. Color pictures are important. Texting is the new medium for connecting with people under 20.
8. Event Focused Worship: Make the most of Christmas and Easter and other special days.
9. Vision Talks Quarterly: Who our church is trying to reach; What we will do to reach them; Where we will reach people; How many will we reach?
10. 21st Century Liturgy: One hour programming; Common language.

SUMMARY

What can we learn from the Highlands Church? Pastor Graham Baird cites two main principles in their ministry: **1. Meeting people where they are.** This involves going to where the people are rather than having them come to you. So they began in a movie theater, had Bible study in a pizza parlor, held meetings for women in a hotel. **2. Learning from our mission field.** The pastor and staff surmised that those who came fell into the following categories: 20% former Baptists; 20% former charismatics; 60% dechurched (persons who had attended church at one time but had left for various reasons). They worked at understanding the backgrounds of the people who attended regarding baptism, music, church polity, style of worship, etc. He believes that Highlands Church should stand firm on orthodox Christianity, but learn a methodology that is appropriate to their mission field. [Pastor Baird feels that the Christian community in Paso Robles of over 40 churches is quite conservative with many of the churches immersed in a rigid fundamentalism. He believes that Highlands Church has found an important niche not common to Paso Robles.] One gets the impression that this church is being enthusiastically supported by the Presbytery of Santa Barbara.

CHAPTER ELEVEN

Korean Good Shepherd Presbyterian Church

1816 Desire Avenue, Rowland Heights, California 91748
626-965-3443; FAX 626-965-0404; E-mail: info@sunhanchurch.com
www.goodshepherdem.com   San Gabriel Presbytery

Exterior of Church Building from Desire Avenue

76% MEMBERSHIP GROWTH, 2002-2007

Year	Members	Gain	%	Lost	%	Wor.Atten	Receipts
2007	913	185	20	15	1.6	927	1,796,500
2002	518	101	19.5	73	14	540	1,119,447
Difference	395	84				387	677,053

Korean Program Schedule:

Sunday Worship
        8:00 a.m.   Traditional
        11:00 a.m.   Blended
        12:50 p.m.   Contemporary

English Program Schedule:

Sunday

9:30 a.m.	English Worship	
	Children's Worship	
11:00 a.m.	Children's and Youth Worship	
12:50 p.m.	Korean School	
Wednesday	8:00 p.m.	Midweek Bible Study & Discipleship
Friday	9:30 p.m.	College Friday Fellowship

PASTORS

Rev. Tae Hyung Ko	Senior Pastor
Rev. Jin Oh Bae EM	Pastor & Education Pastor
Pastor Edward Kim	Senior High Pastor
Pastor Clark Choi	Junior High Pastor
Pastor Michelle Lee	Elementary Pastor
Soo Kyung Hwang	Pre-K and Kindergarten
Soo Young Choi	Nursery

Good Shepherd began in Monterey Park sharing the facilities of the Good Shepherd Presbyterian Church along with Formosan Good Shepherd. The Good Shepherd congregation was dissolved in 1997, and the property was given to the Korean and Taiwanese congregations. In 1992 the Korean congregation reported 120 members. In 1995 Korean Good Shepherd moved to new facilities in Rowland Heights.

In 1995 the property and facilities on Desire Avenue in Rowland Heights were purchased with funds on hand, giving by the congregation, and loan support via the Presbyterian Church (USA). There is a substantial Korean population in Roland Heights and the adjacent communities. The Church recently celebrated its 34th anniversary.

The church property consists of 4.11 acres. It includes a parking lot for 225 cars. Additional parking is available via the nearby Middle School. On a typical Sunday 800-850 people will be attending the four services of worship and 400 of these will be engaged in Sunday Bible study classes. The church holds a Wednesday night worship program including prayer, music, and message. The thirty leaders of the Sunday morning and afternoon small groups attend this program plus two concurrent Bible studies led by Pastor Ko and Pastor Bae. The pastors teach the lesson that the leaders will be teaching in their small groups the following Sunday.

VISION

1. Embraced by God: It all flows out of God's gracious action toward us. He is always reaching down to where we are, and no matter who we are or what we have done, or where we have been, our God takes us by our hands and leads us, through the cross, unto himself with a strong, yet gentle embrace that reminds us all over again, that our God is truly worthy of our worship and service.

2. We worship: And so we worship, not out of obligation, but as a proper expression of our gratitude to our amazing God who lavishes us with amazing grace and love.

3. Grow: And filled with the power of the Holy Spirit, we cannot help but to grow in all ways—through transformative worship and Bible studies, through deeper relationships with our members, through acts of service within the church and without, in reaching out to those near and far away with the love of Christ.

4. Love: Always being reminded that loveless pursuits of knowledge leads to arrogance and loveless acts of service leads to feelings of superiority and power, and loveless relationships leads to tension and strife, we will base all of our actions in love—love for God and love for others.

5. And Proclaim: And above all, remembering the last words of Jesus, that we should bear the name of Jesus Christ and proclaim the Good News in our neighborhoods and to the ends of the earth, we will be outward looking at all times.

Worship Service

We attended the English Worship Service at 9:30 a.m. and the Korean Service at 11:00 a.m. We were impressed with the friendliness and congeniality of the people. A number were anxious to be helpful. An elder escorted us around the church after the 11:00 a.m. service. The English Service was primarily young adults and people in their upper teens. The praise band was very loud with a strong beat and a loud drummer. I presume that those present liked the music. There were about forty to fifty in this service. In addition to the English Service, there are three services in the Korean language: 8:00 a.m. Traditional; 11:00 a.m. Melded; 12:50 p.m. Contemporary.

An elder told me that the church draws its membership from about a ten mile radius. This would primarily include Rowland Heights, Hacienda Heights, Diamond Bar, and Chino Hills. It appears that refreshments of doughnuts and coffee are available between all services. Lunch is served in the patio area following the 11:00 a.m. worship service. A Bible study program is held concurrent with the 12:50 a.m. service involving many young people and leaders.

PROGRAMS
Thirty small groups with a few meeting on Sunday morning and most
    meeting at 12:50 p.m. Sunday afternoon
Korean Language School at 1:00 p.m. on Sundays with thirteen classes
    meeting for 80 minute sessions.
Men's Ministry
Women's Ministry
High School
College

MISSIONS PROGRAMS
Mercy Ministry a comprehensive program of feeding, clothing, helping with housing in the Southern California community. The church dedicated 6% of its budget (about $100,000) to this helping ministry.
Compassion International The church as adopted 300 South American children and expends about $100,000 per year on this ministry.
Presbyterian General Assembly Mission Support.
Pastor Ko studied at the Presbyterian Seminary in Richmond, Virginia, where he received the Doctor of Education degree, and served a Presbyterian Church in Virginia for nine years before responding to the call of Good Shepherd Korean to become their pastor in 2003. He evidences appreciation for the Presbyterian ministry in Korea for the last 140 years.

Sunday Lunch following the 11:00 a.m. Service

SUMMARY

One is impressed with the intentionality of this church in its programs and ministries. Whether it is worship, small groups, men's and women's ministries, missions and outreach. They all comprise a part of a whole in reaching people for Christ, strengthening and training believers in their faith, and helping a bearing witness to the world. This is especially exemplified in the small group program involving about 400 persons per week and in the careful guidance that the pastors give to the leaders.

CHAPTER TWELVE

First Presbyterian Church

830 Padre Drive, Salinas, California 93901
831-422-8160 FAX 831-422-9887 E-mail: imike@fpsalinsa.org
www.fpcsalinas.org San Jose Presbytery

Foyer of new multi-purpose facility

21% MEMBERSHIP GROWTH, 2002-2007

Year	Members	Gain	%	Lost	%	Wor.Atten.	Receipts
2007	2109	108	5	22	1	1634	2,504,564
2002	1736	43	2.5	67	4	779	1,677,743
Difference	373					855	826,821

Sunday School Attendance: Nursery - Junior High = 343

Sunday Worship Services

9:00 a.m.	Contemporary at the Worship Center on Main Street
10:30 a.m.	Alternative Contemporary at the Worship Center on Main
10:45 a.m.	Traditional Service at the Sanctuary on Padre Drive

Sunday School and Youth

9:00 a.m.	3 year olds
10:30 a.m.	Kindergarten
	3rd Grade
	4th/5th Grades
9:00 and 10:30 a.m.	Middle School
10:45 a.m.	High School
7:00 p.m.	College

Over 500 children and 150 adult volunteers participate in Children's Ministry. A full Sunday School program is offered for infants through 5th graders during all Worship Services. A class designed for special needs students ages 8 - 68 years meets during the 10:45 a. m. service. The High School Program is held mid-week with an average attendance of 300. College age have a weekly Bible study during the summer months. Because of their strong youth ministry, they advise Parents: "We will help you raise "G" rated kids in an "R" rated world."

Program Staff

Dr. Mike Ladra, Senior Pastor (since 1987)
Rev. Daryle Bush, Executive Pastor
Taj Hussain, Family Life
Linda Seldmridge, Children's Director
Vern Wetzly, Seniors
Chris Rury, Junior High
Vael Birkins, Senior High/College
Raquel Doolittle, Children's & Spanish Translation
Wang Nelson, Women's Ministries
Laetusu Grey, Children

Media Ministries

Sunday Sermons are broadcast on KKMC (880 AM) Sundays at 8:00 a.m. and 4:00 p.m. and weekdays 6:30 a.m. and 5:30 p.m.
On Television Stations: Channel 35, Sundays at 8:30 a.m. and on Channel 24 Thursdays at 2:30 and 8:30 p.m. and Friday 8:30 a.m.

Activities

Monthly Family Lunches	12:00 to 1:30 p.m.	The Pizza Factory
Couples Bible Studies	Tuesdays, 6:30 p.m.	
New Step Study	Tuesdays, 7:00 p.m.	
Couples Bible Studies	Sundays, 10:30 a.m.	
Couples Bible Studies	Thursdays, 6:30 p.m.	

Pastor Ladra's Evaluation of reasons for growth
1. Devotion to prayer by Elders and Staff, one hour per meeting
2. Our Purposes: Centrality of Jesus and saving the unsaved
3. Perseverance
4. Not trying to reach all people with one style of worship
5. Understanding the importance of music to under 40s
6. Preaching style that is biblical and has take home value
7. The right staff in purpose driven job descriptions
8. Long term pastorate and staff
9. Relationships on staff with each other
10. Example! It's so important to go first
11. Strategic women's ministry as key to evangelism
12. Radio ministry has produced many new members

The agricultural industry around Salinas began to grow in the mid-1800s. In 1867 local businessmen laid out a town plan, and invited the Southern Pacific Railroad to build its tracks through the city. Salinas became the seat of Monterey County in 1872 and incorporated in 1874. The Salinas Valley fuels a two billion dollar agriculture industry which supplies 80% of the nation's lettuce and artichokes, along with many other crops. The current city population is about 150,000 with the population of Monterey County more than 400,000. Demographics: White 59%; Black 2%; Asian 8%; Hispanic 30%; American Indian .8%.

In 1984 membership was 1,593, and the church was averaging just above 300 in worship. "New believers, especially under 40, see no point to membership. They feel part of the church without it." "We do worship for believers but in a manner that allows unbelievers to understand what is being said and done." Nearly 60% of new members in the last eight years have been by conversion. Hundreds of people have attended for three or more years and have not joined. In the last three years worship attendance has more than doubled from 901 to 1,910. In the 1990s there were two traditional services and few young families. In 1997 one service was changed to a contemporary service and began to increase, especially with young families. In 2000 the contemporary service had outgrown the sanctuary and was moved to the gym; it grew rapidly and filled the gym.

The church bought a building a block away from the church property, demolished it, and built a three story building for Sunday School with a 1,500 seat worship center, which was occupied in 2005. Within a year the Contemporary Service filled the new worship center and a second Contemporary Service was begun. One is a more normal contemporary service. The second service is specifically targeted to those in their thirties, and has a more edgy feel and stronger bass line. "At our sanctuary, a block away, we have kept the choir and organ and traditional liturgy but remain seeker-sensitive. Most of the older people enjoy that service, and continue as an important part of the church.

The Salinas church has what it considers to be a lean staff of ten program people. The Senior Pastor and Executive pastor are the only ordained members of the staff. "A long term, happy staff and pastor are an important factor in growth." First Presbyterian Church of Salinas has changed from a slowly declining, traditional, older membership to a multi-campus, multi-ethnic, evangelistic church with a lot of transformation happening.

Excerpts From Pastor Mike Ladra's Web Page Welcome

"We are a purpose-driven fellowship of Christians whose purpose is to change the world through Jesus. The Bible gives a momentous promise: "When someone becomes a Christian, he becomes a brand new person inside. He is not the same anymore. That is the hope for every marriage, every family, every parent, every person who realizes that for the world to change, we need to change. At FPC we have seen Jesus do that again and again in lives.

We are striving to become the kind of church described in the Bible—a place where the focus is a growing personal relationship with Jesus; where there is practical biblical teaching that applies to life; where there is dynamic and uplifting worship; and where there are practical programs for the needs of every age. We are a large, growing church, and the benefit of that to you is that we are big enough for seekers to be inconspicuous among us and big enough to provide a vast array of specialized ministries to people.. Look inside this web site and you will find lots of programs that will help you grow spiritually and live more triumphantly!"

We attended the two Contemporary Services. They are held in the auditorium of the new Worship Center. Both were about an hour and five minutes in length. The first service was a more typical contemporary service; the second service is described as more edgy. However, the only difference is in the music plus strobe lights added to the second service. The order of worship is the same. An offering is received after the pastor's message with only slight emphasis. The traditional service in the church building on Padre Avenue is described as a very typical Presbyterian service with organ and choir. Each of the contemporary services had more than 700 people in attendance. My guess is that the traditional service had, perhaps, 300 in attendance.

74

Stage of new auditorium

The new worship center on Main Street is about a block from the church plant on Padre Avenue. However, there is a clear view from one to the other, and an easy walk for those who want to walk between. The new worship center contains a lower floor for Sunday School and Christian Education purposes. It impresses one as attractive, spacious and very much up to date. The entry to the new building is large with an inviting lobby. Two units of coffee pots provide free coffee and the "Café" sells pastries and also coffee. The auditorium has no windows, with a black ceiling, depending entirely on artificial light. A large stage is in the front with three projection screens above, one in the center and one on each side. They are used for announcements, projecting the words of songs, scripture passages and an occasional phrases or pictures that the pastor wants to use as emphasis. It would be incorrect to say that he uses power point. When we first came into the 9:00 a.m. Contemporary Service, I was struck by the evident professionalism of the music and lighting. I somewhat had the feeling that I should have purchased a ticket! Different praise teams provide the music for each service. The music at the first service is not "country western"—but that's the nearest comparison that I can make. The music at the second service is loud Christian rock. The leaders for each service are paid staff. However, the balance of the musicians are volunteers. It is obvious that they have managed to get volunteers with impressive skills. The addition of the first and then the second Contemporary Service have both resulted in

75

substantial increases in Sunday morning worship attendance. When I told the pastor that if I were to attend regularly, it would be to the 9:00 a.m. service; he said "GOOD". Meaning that the 10:30 a.m. service was not designed for people in my age range! The executive pastor leads the Traditional Worship at 10:45 a.m. in the main church building. The congregation sees Pastor Ladra's message on a large screen. It is obvious that these services get a great deal of care and planning.

SUMMARY

Mike Ladra has been the Senior Pastor of First Presbyterian Church, Salinas for more than twenty years. During that time, in company with the Session and other leaders in the church, he has led the church from a traditional to a multi-faceted ministry that has maintained respect for those who prefer a traditional style worship service. This has been expressed in retaining the traditional church facilities and building a modern multi-use facility a block and a half distant on Main Street. The result includes three distinct worship services, a radio and television ministry, and a variety of programs geared to different ages and different needs. The radio and television ministries have been a major source of newcomers to the church. This church should be a model for churches that want to adapt to current needs without unnecessary disruptions in the congregation.

Sign-ups in Foyer

76

CHAPTER THIRTEEN

San Clemente Presbyterian Church

119 N. Avenida de las Estrerlla, San Clemente, CA 92672
949-492-6158 www.scpres.org Los Ranchos Presbytery

Church Front Entrance and Patio Area

16% MEMBERSHIP GROWTH, 2002-2007

Year	Members	Gain	%	Lost	%	Wor.Atten	Receipts
2007	1311	63	8	27	9	1000	2,124,000
2002	1129	108	13.4	83	10.7	900	1,376,000
Difference	182					100	748,000

Christian Ed. Enrollment: 665

Sunday Worship:

8:00 a.m.	Traditional Service
9:30 a.m.	Traditional Service
11:00 a.m.	Contemporary Service
5:30 p.m.	Contemplative with Communion

Sunday School

9:30 & 11:00 a.m.	Ages 2 ½ through 4th grade; also Class for special needs children Preschool through 4th grade
9:30 -10:30a.m.	Lightforce (5th and 6th grades) Upper Room (Junior High) The Refinery (High School)

Sunday Adult Bible Studies

9:30 a.m.	Estudio Biblio para Adultos
11:00 a.m.	The Book of Proverbs

We attended the 9:30 a.m. melded traditional service and the 11:00 a.m. Contemporary Service. Both services were about an hour in length, although the Contemporary Service began in a more casual manner about 11:07. An organ was in evidence, but was not used in either service. Dual projection screens were at the front of the chancel. They were used for announcements, words for hymns and songs, scripture readings and responses, and to highlight emphases in the pastor's message (concluding a series from the book of Proverbs). Pastor Tod Bolsinger used a small lectern. A large painting of a beautiful tree was in the immediate background and above that a beautiful large multi-colored window. The sanctuary appeared to be completely full for the 9:30 a.m. Traditional (melded) Service and almost full for the Contemporary Service. The pastor was dressed in black short sleeve shirt and tan slacks. The "Bulletin" is the same for both services; the layout is attractive. It includes basic information about the church and information on an impressive number of activities. However, an order of worship is not included.

The order of the 9:30 a.m. service was as follows: Greeting, Announcements, Responsive scripture reading, Songs and Hymns, Prayer of Confession, Offering, Pastoral Prayer with The Lord's Prayer, a Hymn, the message, concluding solo with guitar, and Benediction. There were at least three brief responsive scripture readings during the service. A piano was used for musical accompaniment.

The 11:00 a.m. service was somewhat more casual with a praise band of six persons, leader with guitar who sang, female vocalist, piano, drums, and two more guitarists. The order of worship followed the same pattern as the 9:30 service, but with more music and fewer responsive readings.

The facilities are impressive. The patio layout surrounded by the buildings is exceptional. The church is well located in San Clemente, and quite visible from Interstate 5 to traffic headed south. The Church offers a substantial number of programs including a number that reach out to the community. They sponsor a battalion of Marines at Camp Pendleton, and are active in contacting and caring for them in a number of ways, including a big Christmas party for the families, and a welcome back party when Marines return from overseas.

There was an information booth in the patio and sign-up tables for various programs. An abundance of printed materials were available to pick-up including an impressive "Choral Program Schedule" for September through January indicating the following groups and choirs: Children's Choir, Isaiah Chorus Rehearsal, Praise Band Rehearsal, Sounds of Bronze Bells Rehearsal, Sanctuary Choir Rehearsal, Praise Choir Rehearsal, Christmas Choir Rehearsal, Christmas Program Dress Rehearsal, and Christmas Concert Weekend.

Vision Statement:

San Clemente Presbyterian Church is a "Community for the community", a multigenerational, life transforming, unwaveringly Christ centered Community of people who, together, worship the Triune God, proclaim and demonstrate the Good News of God and provide every person in the greater San Clemente area A place to belong in the family of God, A place to grow in Jesus Christ and A place to serve by the leading and power of the Holy Spirit.

Pastor Bolsinger's Evaluation:

"I have been doing some thinking on the question about what we have done uniquely to contribute to growth and I think I have hit on two particular characteristics that are worth lifting up."

1. A clear set of shared core values. We have a very solid biblically-rooted core of people that have served as the foundation for bringing change. They believe the scriptures, they care about the gospel, and they want to see lives changed. In this sense, while we have a fair amount of diversity, I can't minimize how important it is that San Clemente Presbyterian has a clear set of shared core values. Our identity or ideology, as some have said, is clear, consistent, and has never been a matter of dispute since I have been here. We have been intentional about reaffirming and holding onto that set of shared theological and missional convictions and making decision consistent with them.

2. As we have faced challenges that demanded that we change, we have done so consistent with our code—as Kevin Ford, has defined it in "The Defining Essence of a Church" in his book, *The Transforming Church*. We have been able to frame the most difficult changes and challenges (e.g. a 13 million dollar campus renovation, the addition of a contemporary service, a new Hispanic ministry, a commitment to local mission in addition to foreign missionary support) in terms that reinforced and were congruent with the culture of San Clemente. Until lately, we did not realize how truly important this has been. Now we work really hard to encode everything.

Sanctuary, Contemporary Service

Programs and Activities:
Men's Annual Fishing Classic; Midshipmen Supper Club; J.O.Y. Lunch; Reading Club 205;
Career Transition and Networking Group. Meets every other Wednesday. "Networking + information for successful job search, prayer, support from your church family."
The Ones (Senior Single Ladies 55+) meet the first Monday of each month at 9:00 a.m.
Parkinsons Support Group meets the fourth Tuesday of each month
Grief Support Group meets every Monday 7 - 8:30 p.m

Cancer support Group: A monthly support group for cancer survivors, caregivers, and families. Meets the 2nd Monday each month at 7:00 p.m.

Road Cycling Fellowship: "A friendly group of cyclists, both serious (100+miles/week) and not so serious (20-50 miles/week), who enjoy a great ride twice a week.

First Place 4 Health: "Do you want to lose weight? Have a healthier body? Feel better or have a more balanced life? Join your SCPC friends as we continue on our journey of learning to give Christ first place in every area of our lives, including our bodies!

Walkie Talkies meet the fourth Sunday of each month for walking and fellowship.

Bible Studies: (some of these groups do not meet during July and August)
> Men's Weekly Bible Studies Tuesdays at 7:00 a.m.
> Men's Friday Morning Devotional Group meets for breakfast in a local restaurant, 7:00 a.m.
> Women's Wednesday Morning Bible Study, 9-11 a.m.
> Fall Women's Bible Study
> Women's Circle Groups meet the second Thursday of every month in homes
> Grandmas' Prayer Group, 10:00 a.m. first Thursday of each month

Church Program Staff:

Dr. Tod Bolsinger	Pastor and Head of Staff
David Chavez	Executive Director of Mission & Hispanic Ministries
Garrett Erickson	Associate Pastor of Community Life & Outreach
Rev. Dee Hazen	Associate Pastor of Caring Ministries
Don Nieman	Executive Director of Worship Ministries
Rev. Jim Toole	Associate Pastor of Discipleship & Family Ministries
Rev. Pati Toole	Associate Pastor of Global Mission Partners

Support Staff: Terri Beck, Preschool Asst. Dir.; Diana Castruita, Dir. of Children's Ministries; Brieann Glass, Dir. of High School Ministry, Janet Goode; Asst. to Worship Ministries; Sue Haffely, Asst. to Community Life & Outreach and Caring Ministries; Kelly King, Asst. to Family Ministries and Mission Ministries; Matt King, Facilities Asst.; Becky Knip, Receptionist; Kim Lee-Thorp, Asst. to Dr. Bolsinger; Bob Miller, Facilities Manager; Ryan Romberg, Dir. of Jr. High Ministries; Peter Sedlewicz, Business Manager; Julie Snyder, Dir. of Children's Ministry (Sunday); Dana Spohn, Preschool Dir.; Casey Thomas, Asst. Dir. to Sunday School; Lynda Thomas, Dir. of Worship Prod.; Laura van der Meulen, Communic. Dir.

SUMMARY

The San Clemente Church is an older church that has relatively recently gone through a period of renewal and membership growth. We note the many specialized groups: Career Transition, Walkie Talkies, First Place 4 Health, and a number of others. Their extensive music ministry is obviously vital and important to them. Their special caring and continuing relationship with a Marine battalion and their families at Camp Pendleton is an inspiring example of a ministry outside the church that involves many in the church. The Church Web Site offers the Pastor's Sermons on Line: Download sermon text (PDF) for reading/printing; Listen to the sermon or lecture; Download the sermon or lecture to an MP3 player; Get to the podcast (juice or itunes); Get to our .mobi network to download into your cell phone. A new program is "Big Wednesday": a large evening gathering for all ages offering different opportunities for all ages to engage in spiritual growth and healthy relationships. The San Clemente church continues dynamic in its outlook.

Patio Fellowship between services

CHAPTER FOURTEEN

Grace Presbyterian Church
31134 Nicolas Road, Temecula, California 92591
951-695-1913 E-mail: gracepres.temec@verizon.net
www.gracepreschurch.net   Riverside Presbytery

Front of Grace Presbyterian Church

115% MEMBERSHIP GROWTH, 2002-2007

Year	Members	Gain	%	Lost	%	Wor.Atten	Receipts
2007	433	43	9.9	16	3.7	324	488,473
2002	201	33	16.4	27	13.4	153	233,832
Difference	232					171	254,641

Sunday School Attendance: 200

9:00 a.m.	Contemporary Worship Service
	Nursery, Children's Classes, Pre-K through Grade 5
10:30 a.m.	Traditional Worship Service
	Nursery, Children's Classes; Pre-K through Grade 5
	Middle School, High School, College/Career Classes

PROGRAM AND SUPPORT STAFF

Dr. Earl Stewart	Interim Pastor
David Bazan	Choir Director
Corinne Carey	Church Secretary
Kathy Nelson	Financial Secretary
Marnie Maier	Church School Director

We attended the Contemporary Worship Service at 9:00 a.m. The church does not appear to have an organ. The piano was the primary instrument. The Praise Team consisted of five singers and four instruments: Piano, Drums, Guitar, and Gourds. The songs and hymns were projected on the white wall in back of the Chancel. Projection was not used during the sermon. A feature of this service was the baptism of a very young baby. About eight family and friends came forward to accompany the parents. The pastor took considerable time introducing the family and friends and telling something of the couple's background. It was a heartwarming time.

The service proceeded as follows: Welcome and Announcements; Presentation regarding One Great Hour of Sharing; Praise Song, "Holy Is The Lord; Sacrament of Baptism; Children's Time; Praise Songs, "Better Than", "Lord Listen to Your Children Praying", "What A Friend We Have In Jesus; Invitation to the Offering; Offertory, "More Love, More Power"; Pastoral Prayer and The Lord's Prayer, Scripture, Message, "The Discipline of Prayer!"; Special Music, Temecula Valley Master Chorale; Benediction; Postlude. The pastor was dressed casually. Time: 1 hour, 5 minutes. Attendance 90 - 100.

The Traditional Worship Service was at 10:30 a.m. It included: Gathering Song, "Lord Listen to Your Children Praying"; Welcome and Announcements; Presentation on One Great Hour of Sharing; Introit; Responsive Call to Worship; Children's Time; Hymn, "What a Friend We Have in Jesus"; Confession of Sin; Assurance of Pardon; Gloria Patri; Responsive Reading; Choir Anthem, "Sweet Hour of Prayer"; Pastoral Prayer and the Lord's Prayer; Invitation to the Offering; Offertory; Doxology and Prayer of Dedication; Scripture; Message; Hymn, "More Love to Thee'; Benediction; Postlude. The pastor wore a robe with a stole. The Choir wore robes. "The Hymnal" by Word Publishing. No projection was used during this service. Time: 1 hour, 2 minutes. Attendance 200 - 220.

Coffee, beverages, and refreshments were served in the Patio area between services and after the 10:30 a.m. service. We had time between services to have coffee and cookies and talk with a few people. We had the distinct feeling that this was a friendly congregation, and that they felt very good about their church. At the time they were being led by a very able supply pastor, Dr. Ken McCullen. An interim pastor is expected soon.

REGULARLY SCHEDULED PROGRAMS DURING THE WEEK

Stephen Ministry, Mariner Program, Presbyterian Women (Rebekah Circle, Dorcas Service Group, Abigail Book Group, Moms Group [for mothers and preschool-age children], Sarah Circle, Lydia Bible Study), Adult Education, Youth Ministries: Middle School, High School, College (Summer only); Children's Ministry (Amazing Grace Place!), Worship & Music Ministries: Chancel Choir, Praise Team (Contemporary), Grace Notes (Handbell Choir), Children of Grace (Children's Choir)

Traditional Worship Service in the Sanctuary

MISSION PROGRAMS THAT ARE EMPHASIZED

Temecula & Murrieta Pantries: Support two pantries with money and food and clothing drives

Tecate Mission: Mission teams make the trip to Tecate, Mexico several times a year to work on the facilities

Ronald McDonald House at Loma Linda Hospital

Menaul School

Heifer.org

Christmas Shoebox (Samaritan's Purse)

Angel Tree Prison Ministry

Habitat for Humanity

BACKGROUND

The population of Temecula is about 77,000. The median resident age is 31.3 years compared to a California median of 33.3 years. The median household income is about $72,000 compared to a California median of about $60,000. The racial makeup of Temecula: White (Non-Hispanic), 69.3%; Hispanic 19%; Other 7.4%; Two or more races 4.4%; Black 3.4%; Filipino 2.7%; American Indian 1.7%

The city of Temecula, located at the southwest corner of Riverside County was incorporated in 1989. Riverside, California is 36 miles to the northeast, and San Diego is 50 miles south. A housing boom took place as people relocated to a land of ranches and vineyards. In 1990, Merly Goodpaster, a Presbyterian elder and member of the Riverside Presbytery New Church Development Committee was a new resident in Temecula and recognized the need for a Presbyterian Church. The area had fifty churches of which only five had their own church building. Most were located in commercial or industrial or school buildings available for a few hours on Sundays.

The Rev. John A Flahiff became the first organizing Pastor in August, 1990. The worship services were held in the Sparkman Elementary School beginning 2 February 1991. Initially, church attendance was good with two Sunday Services, children's ministry and fellowship activities for all age groups. Good lay leadership was appearing. During this time Pastor Flahiff was greatly involved in purchasing land for church construction. From 1990 through 1993 the economy in the Temecula area weakened including a downturn in housing prices. Many persons lost their jobs—and many of the people and leaders in the church left for a variety of reasons.

The years 1993-1994 brought new lay leadership to the church. The Riverside Presbytery continued its financial support. The economy began to improve, however church membership was about fifty and the church was not financially solvent. 1 February 1996 the Rev. John Chambers became the organizing pastor. The name, Grace Presbyterian Church, was adopted, and the church was chartered 18 May 1997.

On 1 July 2000 the Rev. Jerry Hangen became pastor. New property was purchased in 2001, and a building committee formed in 2002. The first phase of construction was completed and the new multipurpose building was in use in March, 2006. By the end of 2006, the congregation had grown to more than 400 members with 12 full and part time staff.

GRACE PRESBYTERIAN STATEMENT OF FAITH

We believe in God the Father, maker of heaven and earth. We believe in Jesus Christ, His only Son, as our Lord and Savior. He died for our sins and reigns today in heaven and one day will come again to judge all the world. We believe in His Holy Spirit as our guiding strength in the world today and the power that guides and directs Christ's Church in all times. We believe the Bible is the authoritative Word of God and the true witness to Jesus Christ in the world today. We believe the Church is God's instrument for nurture, fellowship, mission, instruction, evangelism, and a house of worship that welcomes all.

Coffee Fellowship at the Front Entrance

SUMMARY

The people in Grace Church appear to excel in ministering to one another. The Deacons have an impressive program of parish area care. They call on every person in their assigned parish monthly, and fill out a form on each call for the pastor to read. The deacon's ministry is complimented by a strong Stephen Ministry program. The Tecate Mission is a unifying force. They possess a high quality of lay leadership, and are strong in their faith in Jesus Christ. They appear to be open to new directions in which God will lead them.

CHAPTER FIFTEEN

Westminster Presbyterian Church

32111 Watergate Road; Westlake Village, California 91361
818-889-1491 FAX 818-889-7132
www.wpcwestlake.org   Presbytery of San Fernando

Patio prior to worship

8% MEMBERSHIP GROWTH, 2002-2007

Year	Members	Gain	%	Lost	%	Receipts
2007	1146	73	6	68	6	1,526,547
2002	1063	63	6	72	7	1,010,386
Difference	83					516,161

Sunday School Attendance: 150 (Beginners - Sixth Grade)

Ministry Staff:
Rev. Dr. Richard H. Thompson, Pastor
Rev. John F. Burnett, Parish Associate
Rev Jennifer Kates Witten, Parish Associate
17 other staff members, full and part-time
The Church is seeking a full time Associate Pastor

Sunday Worship Schedule:

8:30 a.m.	Traditional worship in the Sanctuary
10:00 a.m.	Traditional worship in the Sanctuary
11:15 a.m.	Contemporary worship in the Fellowship Center
10:00 a.m.	Sunday School for Children and Youth
	High School Sunday School
	Adult Sunday School
11:15	Adult Sunday School

In 1963 the American-Hawaiian Steamship Company in partnership with the Prudential Insurance Co. bought a 12,000 acre ranch, and developed a master plan for a "city in the country", which became the City of Westlake Village. It was incorporated in 1981. The population is about 9,000. It is 38 miles west of downtown Los Angeles.

We attended the 10:00 and 11:15 a.m. worship services. Both services were about an hour and five minutes in length. The 10:00 a.m. service was traditional with the following order: Prelude; Introit; Call to Worship and Prayer; Hymn, "Great Is Thy Faithfulness"; Prayer of Confession; Gloria Patri; Children's Message; Offering, Offertory, Doxology, Prayer; Scripture; Hymn of Preparation; Second Scripture; Sermon; Hymn, "And Can It Be That I Should Gain?"; Pastoral Prayer and the Lord's Prayer; Benediction; Choral Response; Postlude. About 34 members in the Choir and about 30 children present for the Children's Message. The 8:30 a.m. service used the same schedule except there was no children's message.

The Contemporary Service had a much simpler liturgy: Praise Singing; Scripture; Children's Message; Second Scripture Reading; Sermon; Pastoral Prayer; Offering; Benediction; Postlude (Instrumental jazz rendition). Another substantial group of children present for the Children's Message. The Contemporary Service is held in the Fellowship Center with two large screens projecting the words to the songs. The Praise Team was composed of five males, three guitarists, a drummer, and a keyboard. Everyone present participated in the singing.

The church has a large and inviting courtyard surrounded by the church buildings. The congregation obviously enjoys the conversation and refreshments. The Pastor, Dr. Richard H. Thompson is a graduate of UC Santa Barbara with a major in French literature. He received the M.Div. from Fuller Seminary and the D. Min. from San Francisco Seminary.

Ongoing Scheduled Events:

Junior High Youth Fellowship	Tuesdays	6:00 p.m.
Ministry to Young Adults	Tuesdays	7:45 p.m.
Gathering in Grace for Women	Wednesdays	9:30 a.m.
Balanced Wednesdays (for Seniors)	Wednesdays	9:30 a.m.
Includes Conversation, Exercise, and Lunch		
Westminster Free Clinic	Wednesdays	5:00 p.m.
Homeless Shelter Meals	Wednesdays	6:30 p.m.
The Decaffeinated Word for Men	Wednesdays	7:00 p.m.
Bible Study for Senior High Students	Wednesday	7:00 p.m.
Mothers of Young Children	Wednesdays	8:00 p.m.
Chancel Choir Rehearsal	Thursdays	7:30 p.m.
Couple's Bible Study	Saturdays	7:00 p.m.

Traditional Worship Service in the Sanctuary

The Church conducts three church membership classes each year. Ordinarily, on a Friday evening and the following Saturday morning.
Confirmation Class (9th - 12th grade) Sundays 8:30 a.m.
"If someone asked you why you go to church, what would you say? Have you ever had any questions about God? Do you wonder why active participation in church is important? Have you ever wanted to know who Jesus was? Would you like to know what makes the Christian faith different form other world religions?" The class culminates with an opportunity for baptism and church membership for those who are interested.

FIVE CORE VALUES:

1. Worshiping Church: WPC gathers in three worship services each Sunday morning, at 8:30, 10:00 and 11:15. Each service of worship, though unique in style, offers an invitation to encounter our Lord's risen presence. The 8:30 and 10:00 services meet in the Sanctuary. The 11:15 service meets in the Fellowship Center.

2. Inviting Church: WPC is known in the region of the Conejo Valley for its warmth of welcome to anyone searching for a good place to call "home." Overlapping systems of outreach, invitation, greeting and introduction facilitate a process of assimilating a first-time visitor into active participation.

3. Caring Church: Every member and friend of WPC who has attended for two months or more is a part of a "web of caring." A network of small caring, support, and discipleship groups provide each one a way to build in-depth friendship. An active array of men's, women's and family ministries provides an easy entry point for new and long-term members alike.

4. Learning Church: WPC is known in the community for the quality of its classes, seminars, workshops, retreats and small groups for growing Christian of all ages. Families discover thematically interwoven subjects in the Learning Church from preschool to adults throughout the week. WPC's preschool gives expression to the vision of WPC's mission in engaging ways which help young families take their "next step" in Christian growth and discipleship. Children, youth and adults learn what it means to be "fully devoted followers of Jesus Christ" both through scripturally based content and training in the disciplines of community life. "Family Matters" classes and events are offered continuously. WPC's ministry with youth takes in a ten-year span from 10 to 20 years of age, and also includes a ministry with these families.

5. Gift-Evoking Church: There is a "core" of members and friends at WPC who can articulate the vision, core values, their own place in the process of Christian discipleship and their "next step" in that process. "Leadership development" utilizes a strategy of aligning giftedness with areas of ministry in need of those gifts. An Office for Lay Ministry coordinates interviews, requests, and training events to under-gird SPC's ever-growing number of ministries both inside (worship, music, theater, teaching, caring, leading, hospitality, etc.) and outside the walls (community organizing, evangelism, advocacy, compassion, justice, peacemaking, cross-cultural outreach, etc.). Gift-evoking manifests itself in an increasing commitment to mission beyond the walls, both in budget and "hands-on" ministry involvement.

Contemporary Service in the Fellowship Center

SUMMARY
Most of these growing churches seem to work within a framework of seventy minutes of worship services although a few will go as long as an hour and a half. It is possibility that the relative brevity of these services makes at least a small contribution to their growth success. Perhaps, a better way to put it is that they indicate a discipline in time use. For example, if they have a special interview or missionary presentation they reduce something else in the service to compensate.

CHAPTER SIXTEEN

LOOKING AT WHAT WE HAVE SEEN

How can we learn from what we have read and seen of these churches? We may congratulate them on the strength and success of their ministries—but what of many other churches? I do not think that we discern a common template that fits them all, and that can be applied to every church. There are notable differences in geographic location, membership, age of the church, building facilities, style of worship, and program emphases. That should, in a sense, be encouraging because if we could attribute their strengths to a single overall factor we might well say that is good—but it does not pertain to our situation—therefore, what we see and learn will be of no help to us.

We cannot attribute the growth of most of these churches to the fact that they are in growing areas. They have distinguished themselves from churches in similar circumstances. The membership of the Presbytery of San Gabriel is about one third of what it was when formed in 1968[1] while the population of the area has more than doubled. Population growth does not guarantee church growth, but we can learn from one another. On the other hand, in our examples and suggestions—we certainly do not want to be like Procrustes, who stretched out or amputated his victims to fit a standard iron bed! There are a variety of ways that churches can improve.

What we see here are fifteen churches in California that are notably successful in reaching out to the communities of which they are a part. Perhaps, most important, we see Presbyterian churches growing in numbers in a denomination that is declining in membership. What is possible for these churches should be possible for many other churches. One of these churches is very new: the Highlands Church in Paso Robles. Several of them have been new church developments within the past fifteen years or so: Clovis, Temecula, St. Peters by-the-Sea in Huntington Beach, Rowland Heights Korean. Others are older well established churches that have gone through an impressive renewal.

---

[1] San Gabriel Presbytery Communicant Membership, 1968 = 30,823; 2007 = 10,016

To the degree that some of these churches manifest an exceptional gathering of talent or an almost magical sense of harmony and unity—there may well be aspects about them that others cannot obtain. But what of the successful growth and adaptability of the Salinas Church? What of the attention given to small groups by the Bel Air church? What of the careful attention given to the development of their worship services by most of these churches? One thing I especially noted in visiting these churches is the high quality of the preaching. Cannot most of us, who preach, elevate our preaching to a stronger level? Again, we note that they are diligent in caring for their facilities, both exterior and interior. They show a predictable concern for people who need to believe in Jesus Christ. This concern is a primary factor driving everything else in the congregation. Related to that concern is a commitment to help in various forms of mission, both evangelism and in a variety of helping ministries, that involve substantial numbers of people in these churches, not only in financial support, but in their personal participation. These participatory programs appear to be a powerful magnet to draw a congregation together.

What we have called the mainline denominations are really not the mainline anymore: Presbyterian, Methodist, United Church of Christ, Lutheran, many Baptists, etc. The notable growth is with the Southern Baptists, Pentecostals, and independent Evangelicals. There are a number of reasons for the decline of the mainline churches, but here is a for-instance: Until recently the Presbyterian and Reformed Churches have had the basic sanctuary structure and order of style of worship that originated with John Calvin and John Knox in the 16th century. Now there happen to be parts of these structures and styles that many of us like—but that was at a time when the average Protestant or Protestant leaning person was familiar with the Bible and with the traditional music of the church. That is no longer true of the general population. One characteristic of the growing churches is that they have not been so hide-bound. Another problem is that many mainliners have lost their nerve regarding the authority of the Bible. Yes, there are things in the Bible that people may not like. But the message of the Bible supports our main product. People may not be interested if they find out that we are going into another business.

From 1965 to the present the Presbyterian Church (USA) and most "mainline denominations" have been losing members. The result is that many denominations, and their member churches, have developed a culture of expecting decline. Added to that is a tendency to justify the decline.

(There are, of course, situations with very good reasons for a local church to be declining in membership) So we pat ourselves on the back for being more prophetic than others. Or we say we are eliminating the deadwood so that we can be like Gideon's army. Or we say that we are more faithful in challenging our people and not comforting them. Any one of these may be true. On the other hand, they may just be poor excuses.

What specifically should the Presbyterian Church (USA) do?

1. Clearly acknowledge that evangelism and outreach is the primary purpose of the local church, the Presbytery, and the General Assembly.

2. Train all members in Bible content, and in dealing with common objections—so that when they are encouraged to be witnesses they understand the message that is to be conveyed. Continual training is vital, because we quickly forget, and peripheral things may monopolize the attention of our minds.

3. Understand the basic requirements for church growth. The average Presbyterian Church loses seven per cent of its members annually. This is from three causes: death, relocation, and dissatisfaction. Thus, to maintain the current membership, the church needs to receive seven percent of its membership as new members every year. And to see an increase in membership it must receive more than seven percent of its membership annually.

4. Replace the Per Capita Assessment. The motivation is not to reduce the income of the national church. But we have for too long provided an economic incentive to take people off of the church rolls. Since most of the support for our churches and Presbyteries, and General Assembly causes comes from voluntary contributions—is it not possible that the needs represented by the Per Capita Assessment could be provided in the same way? This would not preclude setting fourth guidelines regarding the needs of higher judicatories. But it would remove the temptation to preemptively remove the alleged "dead wood." We should not remove anyone from church membership rolls who continue to live in our communities unless 1) they are participating in another church or 2) they specifically request to be removed from the membership roll.

5. Follow the instructions of the Book of Order[2] regarding members who are no longer participating. This clearly implies careful pastoral work by ministers and elders in caring for the wayward sheep.

SOME ADDITIONAL REFLECTIONS

It has been a privilege for me to experience and learn from these fifteen churches. Out of that experience I would like to share some of my convictions that I hope will provoke your thinking and be helpful. Is it your intent and purpose in the Saturday evening or Sunday worship service to reach the unconverted, the unchurched, the dechurched, the unbelieving? If that is the case, then we should have these people in mind at every one of our public, open, worship services. With the unchurched in mind, I want to suggest that there are some things that are inappropriate for us to do. I simply offer this for you to think about. "If the shoe fits, then wear it." I realize that what may be inappropriate in one situation may be quite appropriate in another. With that said—here are some "do nots" to consider.

1. Don't ask people to break into small groups for prayer or confession in the Sunday worship service. That is not what your visitor bargained for. He or she understands this to be a public service where everyone is welcome. (I don't mean to imply that we have any secret or restricted meetings, but the major worship services of the week are the ones where visitors are most likely to attend.)

2. Don't put tags on newcomers. If you really want to meet them, find more subtle ways to accomplish this. I realize that in the mega church this may be a problem, but in many churches regular attenders should recognize people that are new or near new and engage them in warm conversation without making them feel that they just arrived from outer space.

3. Don't insult your customers by telling them not to participate in the offering. If properly presented, most new people will understand that it is a freewill offering. They may understand quite clearly that it is something that they offer to God, and that the local church is simply the instrument. Now, I am referring to the regular Sunday morning offering. However, if

---

[2] *The Constitution of the Presbyterian Church (U.S.A.)*, Part II, Book of Order, 0.0302a

you are making a special appeal for the building fund, or for a special missionary cause, or for a Deacons' type ministry—you may want to make it clear that this is exceptional.

4. Don't ask people to hold hands. This is fine for friends and for people who are comfortable with each other. It may not be welcomed by people who really don't know you.

5. And what about the way that we present the Lord's Supper? Is intinction the best way for the newcomer? or for that matter, for the rest of us? I have offered communion in this manner, but I really think that it is second best. It seems to me that people should be free to receive the elements or not. If we ask people to stand up and walk to a station and receive the elements we may be unwittingly coercing people, who feel embarrassed to stay in their seat while everyone else goes forward. I think there is a lot to be said for offering the bread and the wine or the juice on a tray where receiving the elements is much more individual and personal. The Lord's Supper is the most personal, individual, part of the worship service. While I believe that the sacraments should certainly be under the authority of the church—it is not Roman Catholic, Anglican, Baptist or Presbyterian. We simply make the offer on Christ's behalf. It is Jesus offering his body and blood to whomever will receive him. If the unconverted person understands that when the bread and the cup are offered and received—he or she is acknowledging Jesus Christ as Savior, then don't restrict them. The proper offering of the Lord's Supper is, perhaps, one of the best instruments that we have to invite people to receive Jesus Christ.

SOME FINAL THOUGHTS

The entirety of the Bible, but especially the New Testament is emphatic that the Christian is to share the good news, that he or she has received, with others:

Matthew 28:19,20, "Go therefore and make disciples of all nations, baptizing them in the name of the Father and of the Son and of the Holy Spirit, and teaching them to obey everything that I have commanded you. And remember, I am with you always, to the end of the age."

Acts 1:8, "But you will receive power when the Holy Spirit has come upon you; and you will be my witnesses in Jerusalem, in all Judea and Samaria, and to the ends of the earth."

It is instructive that these commandments came shortly before or at the time of Jesus' departure from Earth. Taking the word of God to other people is the highest of priorities. It is also instructive that when we turn to the book of Acts this is exactly what his disciples did. Those who had been closest to Jesus clearly understood what their business was.

Acts 20:24, "But I do not account my life of any value nor as precious to myself, if only I may accomplish my course and the ministry which I received from the Lord Jesus, to testify to the gospel of the grace of God." (RSV)

We note in the second, third, and fourth centuries, the writings and tireless efforts of many Christians to explain Jesus Christ to a pagan world, and to rebut criticisms that had been raised against the Christian community. To mention a few out of a much larger number: Ignatius, Justin Martyr, Irenaeus, Clement of Alexandria, Tertullian, Origin, Augustine of Hippo. And then the names of dedicated and heroic missionaries that were on the front lines of Christian expanse from the fifth to the fifteenth centuries: Augustine, Columba, Columban, Patrick, Boniface, Bernard, et. al.

In spite of the Islamic incursions in the seventh through the fifteenth centuries, the church continued to grow especially northward and westward—and then across the Atlantic to the new world—and eastward into Asia. Today approximately one-third of the world's population identify themselves as Christians. It is the fruit of believers who clearly understood Christ's purpose for them! Ultimately this is the work of the Holy Spirit.

From the beginning Christians have been powerful in making the case for faith in Christ and in seeking to remove the obstacles to belief. The number of churches in the United States that are exemplary in baptizing significant numbers of people in the name of Christ remind us that the fields continue to be "white unto harvest" in this nation. There is continuing need for effective proclamation of the message of our Lord in the United States as well as in the rest of the world. Every church has the opportunity to reach out not only to its own community, but to the rest of the world. We note in these fifteen churches not only a burden to bring Christ to those nearby, but also engagement in supporting the extension of the gospel in other places.

Every local church must resist the temptation to rest on its past victories and become a contented caretaker for the assembled Christians. We can become tightly wrapped up in ourselves in just ministering

98

exclusively to our given group. Again a caveat: we, of course, must teach, exhort, and encourage one another, but we must always be reaching beyond our church. We need to be enriched by the new life that new Christians bring into our fellowship. We can learn from other churches. We need to resist the temptation to become insular and ignore what others are doing. A corollary fault is thinking that our ministry is so unique and correct; that there is nothing that others can teach us. Kevin Ford reflects on the tendency to ignore what others are doing:

> Sadly, the entrenched territorialism of the former leaders had kept their own leadership realms isolated and impoverished. Their pride and possessiveness kept great treasures unknown and unlocked. All it took to unlock them was the humility of asking.[3]

Our theology needs to be rooted in the New Testament and historic Christianity. It must flow out of the Apostles' and Nicene Creeds. And through the Ecumenical Councils that affirmed the full deity of Father, Son, and Holy Spirit, and that clarified the boundaries regarding the nature of Jesus Christ as opposed to Nestorianism and Monophysitism—and subsequently filled out by the major creeds of Protestantism. We must proclaim what the mainstream of the church has proclaimed from the first century to the present.

We should not be searching for new theologies—but for better ways to advocate what we have already received. The temptation is to refine Christian theology so that it accommodates to the world at large. We need a clarified and renewed theology. We don't need to add more so much as we need to continually affirm what we have always believed. We must continually re-encounter the scriptures so that by them we are corrected, encouraged, and strengthened. We need, in love, to continue the process of distinguishing between the essentials of the faith—and those matters that are important but not essential. Surely an indication of Christian love is a willingness to accept fellow Christians who have differing viewpoints.

Has much of the church lost its way? Has maintenance and preservation become the reason for existing? The church is surely the only institution whose primary purpose is for those who are not yet members. A renewed study of Whitfield and Wesley will be worthwhile. They were

---

[3]Ford, Kevin, *Transforming Church*, page 252.

innovators. They were faithful priests in the Church of England—but by trial and error recognized that there were many who did not fit the culture of that church, so they took the preaching of the gospel outside the walls of the church. In a different way that is what we are seeing in many of these growing churches today. They have restructured their ministries to reach the unchurched and the dechurched without destroying effective ministries that have been at the core of their church lives.

We need to be faithful to the scriptures, on the one hand, but we need also to be answering the questions that people are asking. For example: Why is God so distant? Why does God deal with us so harshly? Why does God allow evil to be so rampant? Why do many intelligent people reject Christianity? We need to deal with the perplexities that face people in society at the present time: How do I provide a wholesome atmosphere for my children? How do we provide for the things that we need without going overboard on accumulation of non-essentials? How do I deal with the fear of illness? How do we discern between worthwhile and worthless or harmful entertainment? How do we participate effectively in society at large?

John 8:31,32, "If you **continue in my word**, you are truly my disciples, and you will know the truth, and the truth will make you free."

I Peter 3:15, "Always **be prepared** to make a defense to any one who calls you to account for the hope that is in you, yet do it with gentleness and reverence:"

II Timothy 2:15, "**Do your best** to present yourself to God as one approved, a workman who has no need to be ashamed, rightly handling the world of truth."

Finally, these are just some things to think about, when it is our firm desire to welcome the stranger and newcomer in our midst. First and foremost we want to worship God and honor him, and is that not also what we offer to those who come to us for the first time? My study of these fifteen churches has been a growing and learning experience for me. I hope that it will be for you as well.

But thanks be to God, who in Christ always leads us in triumph, and through us spreads the fragrance of the knowledge of him everywhere. (II Corinthians 2:14, RSV)

BIBLIOGRAPHY

Cootsona, Gregory S., "The Church of the Last Stop" (The Story of Bidwell Presbyterian Church), Geneva Press.

Dallimore, Arnold A., *George Whitfield: God's Anointed Servant in the Great Revival of the Eighteenth Century*, Crossway Books.

Ford, Kevin G., *Transforming Church* (Bringing out the good to get to great), David C. Cook.

Gladwell, Malcolm, *The Tipping Point* (How Little Things Can Make a Big Difference), Little Brown and Company.

Howard, Philip K., *Life Without Lawyers* (Liberating Americans From Too Much Law), W. W. Norton & Company. See chapters five and six for valuable thinking on personnel policies.

Mullin, Robert Bruce, *A Short World History of Christianity*, Westminster John Knox Press.

Murrow, David, *Why Men Hate Going To Church*, Thomas Nelson.

Presbyterian Church (USA), Research Services. An abundance of information on the denomination and individual churches. [www.pcusa.org/research/statistics]

Stenzer, Ed and Dodson, Mike, *Comeback Churches*, B & H Publishing Group.

THE TOP FIFTEEN PRESBYTERIAN CHURCHES IN
MEMBERSHIP GAIN (CALIFORNIA) 2002-2007

Highlands Church (Presbyterian), Paso Robles   467 %
(new church development), 2006-2008, Graham Baird

Grace Presbyterian, Temecula   115 %
     Earl Stewart

Rowland Heights Korean Presbyterian   76 %
     Tae Hyung Ko, Jin Oh Bae

Bidwell Presbyterian, Chico   53 %
     Steve Schibsted, Greg Cootsona, Jeff Gaphart

Bel Air Presbyterian, Los Angeles   45 %
     Mark Brewer, Roger Dermody, Glenn Reph
     Carolyn Crawford, George Hinman

Trinity Presbyterian, Clovis   27 %
     Chuck Shillito, Don Harris

Shepherd of the Sierras, Loomis   23 %
     David Ratcliff

Healdsburg Presbyterian   19%
     Dave Jordan-Irwin, Becca Jordan-Irwin

San Clemente Presbyterian   16%
     Tod Bolsinger, David Chavez, Garrett Erickson

First Presbyterian, Honolulu   15 %
     Dan Chun, David Stoker

Christ Presbyterian, Huntington Beach   15 %
     Gary Watkins, William Welch

First Presbyterian, Salinas   15 %
    Mike Ladra, Daryle Bush

St. Peter's By the Sea, Huntington Beach   14 %
    Chris Grange

Irvine Presbyterian, Irvine   13 %
    Rick Hull, Kirk Winslow, Tim Avezian

Westminster, Westlake   8 %
    Richard H. Thompson, John Burnett

Appendix

FIFTEEN CHURCHES, PASTOR'S TENURE

CHURCH	PASTOR	START	YEARS
Bidwell Presbyterian, Chico	Steve Shibsted	1998	11
Trinity Presbyterian, Clovis	Chuck Shillito	1997	12
Healdsburg Presbyterian	David & Becca Jordan-Irwin	1998	11
Honolulu, First Presbyterian	Dan Chan	1994	15
Huntington Beach, Christ Presbyterian	Gary Watkins	1987	22
Huntington Beach, St. Peter's By the Sea	Chris Grange	2002	7
Irvine Presbyterian	Mark Roberts[1]	1991-1997	16
Loomis, Shepherd of the Sierras	David Ratcliff	1995	14
Los Angeles, Bel Air Presbyterian	Mark Brewer	2001	8
Paso Robles, Highlands Church	Graham Baird	2006	3
Rowland Heights, Korean Presbyterian	Tae Hyung Ko	2003	6
Salinas, First Presbyterian	Mike Ladra	1988	21
San Clemente Presbyterian	Tod Bolsinger	1997	12
Temecula, Grace Presbyterian	Jerry Hangen[2]	2000-2008	8
Westlake, Westminster Presbyterian	Richard Thompson	1996	13

Average Tenure = 12 Years

---

[1]Currently served by Interim Pastor, Rick Hull

[2]Currently served by Interim Pastor, Earl Stewart

PRESBYTERIAN CHURCH (USA) MEMBERSHIP   1960-2007

	MEMBERS	GAIN/LOSS	PERCENT
1960	4,158,127		
1965	4,254,597	+96,470	2.3%
1970	4,049,391	-205,206	4.8%
1975	3,544,099	-505,292	12.5%
1980	3,272,518	-291,842	8.2%
1985	3,057,226	-215,292	4.0%
1990	2,856,713	-200,513	6.6%
1995	2,665,276	-191,437	6.7%
2000	2,525,330	-139,946	5.3%
2005	2,313,662	-211,668	9.1%
2007	2,209,546	-104,116	(2 years)

SOME INTERESTING STATISTICS ABOUT THE PRESBYTERIAN CHURCH (USA)

Membership	Members	Churches
1601 or more	12%	1%
1201-1600	7%	1%
801-1200	10%	2%
501-800	14%	5%
301-500	17%	9%
201-300	12.5%	11%
0-200	27.5%	71%

19% of the churches have 60% of the members

29% of the churches have 72.5% of the members

71% of the churches have 27.5% of the members

Data based on article by Ida Smith-Williams, *Presbyterians Today*, November, 2008

ACKNOWLEDGMENTS

First, I want to thank my dear wife, Janis, for her support and encouragement. She accompanied me on visits to almost all of the churches, and was a big help with the photography, and gave valuable suggestions. I am indebted to Ruth Elliott and her daughter, Lisa, for invaluable help in the final preparation of the text and the insertion of pictures. The Rev. Jim Stochl and Dr. John Chandler were of great help in their comments and criticisms. Also my thanks to the churches that furnishing one or more of the photos in the book. And thanks to the pastors and staffs of these churches without whose generous cooperation this book would not have been possible.

Our gratitude to the family of Marjorie Ward for making a substantial gift in her memory that was an undergirding for this project.

Foster H. Shannon

RECOMMENDATIONS

"The decline of the PC (USA) has been a concern for many people for a number of years. This book has the courage to show us how growing churches are responding to the challenge to reverse the decline. These churches inspire us to take our eyes off of ourselves and the glory days of yesteryear, and to see God's call for the local church to be the fulfillment of God's mission around us. These churches are the specialists in our denomination who have understood their context. Presbyterians are always looking for good models of church growth. I recommend this resource to inspire our churches to never be the same." Rev. Eric Hoey, Director for Evangelism and Church Growth, Presbyterian Church (USA)

"This is one of the most challenging books I have read. It is mind blowing: fifteen growing "thriving"Presbyterian churches out of 540 in California. What strikes me about all of them is that first, they are vitally Christocentric; second, they are truly Reformed, in a sense of the openness and holistic character in their presentation of the gospel in both a personal and societal sense; third, they are adequately funded, most showing great stewardship growth; and finally, most are superbly staffed with excellent ordained preachers, usually teamed with talented, committed lay professionals. This is a book that should receive wide readership." Dr. John Chandler, New Church Development Consultant

"Why These Presbyterian Churches are Growing" gives a snapshot of the varied visions, ministries and methods that are guiding some of our denomination's most vibrant congregations. This book is laid out like a travel guide with statistics, program overviews, ministry highlights and statements of vision and values for most congregations. This will be a very useful resource for pastors and church leaders to 'seed' their strategic thinking. It will generate ideas and will, hopefully, even stimulate direct conversations with the leadership of the congregations presented." Dr. Douglas J. Rumford, Senior Pastor, Trinity United Presbyterian Church, Santa Ana , CA .